A Boy of Old Japan

R. Van Bergen

Alpha Editions

This edition published in 2021

ISBN : 9789355754547

Design and Setting By
Alpha Editions
www.alphaedis.com
Email - info@alphaedis.com

As per information held with us this book is in Public Domain.
This book is a reproduction of an important historical work. Alpha Editions uses the best technology to reproduce historical work in the same manner it was first published to preserve its original nature. Any marks or number seen are left intentionally to preserve its true form.

Contents

PREFACE	- 1 -
I JAPAN ASLEEP	- 2 -
II THE OLD YASHIKI	- 6 -
III THE MESSENGER	- 10 -
IV THE FIFTH DAY OF THE ELEVENTH MONTH	- 15 -
V THE COUNCIL OF THE CLAN	- 19 -
VI YOUNG KANO GROWS UP	- 23 -
VII KANO'S JOURNEY TO YEDO	- 27 -
VIII YOKOHAMA IN 1859	- 31 -
IX NEW EXPERIENCE	- 36 -
X FRIENDSHIP OR HATRED?	- 40 -
XI CHOSHIU'S YASHIKI	- 44 -
XII SONNO-JOI	- 48 -
XIII PLOTTING	- 53 -
XIV WITHIN THE PALACE	- 58 -
XV UNDERGROUND RUMBLING	- 62 -
XVI THE COURT AROUSED	- 66 -
XVII A CONFERENCE	- 70 -
XVIII FLIGHT	- 75 -

XIX BATTLE AND DEFEAT	- 80 -
XX DRILLING	- 84 -
XXI DOWN WITH TOKUGAWA!	- 88 -
XXII CONCLUSION	- 92 -
NOTES	- 98 -
FOOTNOTES:	- 103 -

PREFACE

I AM under deep obligations to the publishers, for giving me an opportunity to tell the story of the rejuvenation of Japan. I was a witness, although at that time I did not comprehend the movement, but I, and those few who are still living, do now.

From a federation of mutually autonomous oligarchies, Japan was metamorphosed into an Empire which holds Russia at bay. From a nation occupying 150,000 square miles, it has expanded by the addition of Formosa, and its population has grown from thirty millions to forty-five millions. An oriental people adopted occidental progress, and within three decades or little more than one generation, digested and assimilated our progress.

I have known, and was personally known to the men, whose story I have endeavored to tell. They are now honored under the simple name of Genrô,—statesmen of Revolutionary Times. Of the brilliant array of patriots whose names appear in these pages, only Ito, Inouye, and OKuma remain!

I have kept the names. Why should I not? Only honor can be bestowed upon such patriots as they; and the world delights to honor them. Besides, there is a healthy spirit for the young in a *true* story of devotion, sacrifice, and self-restraint. How often does a child, when reading an interesting story, ask: "Papa, is this true?" In this case the father may conscientiously answer: It is.

All the characters as portrayed in these pages, were living actors in the great national drama. Of those whose names have never before appeared in print, Karassu Maru, the only *impulsive* noble I have ever known, was the first imperial governor of Yedo. He died in August, 1872, and I attended his funeral. Honami came to Yedo with the emperor, but he was soon sent back to Kyoto, where he was placed under guardianship.

I have enjoyed the retrospective communication with my old friends. If my readers do so, they owe the pleasure to the publishers, who suggested the composition of the book.

R. VAN BERGEN.

CAMBRIDGE, MASS., *Nov. 12, 1900.*

I
JAPAN ASLEEP

JAPAN had been asleep for more than two hundred years. About the time when the Pilgrim fathers landed in what is now known as the New England States, the man who ruled over Japan had made up his mind that he would have nothing more to do with the people of Europe, and he gave orders that no more foreigners should be admitted. He made one exception in favor of the people of Holland, but on condition that only a very small number of them should reside in Japan at a time; and they must be satisfied with the tiny island of Deshima[1] in the harbor of Nagasaki,[2] and promise that they would obey the governor of that city.

It was not many years before this time, when the Japanese had been glad to receive every European, but they had found out that the Portuguese and Spaniards wished to be masters of their country, and so their kindness had changed first into dislike and afterwards into hate. The Portuguese had taught many Japanese about our Lord, and a number of them had become Christians. But the Shogun[3] ordered that all Christians must be killed, and thousands of them were put to death. He gave also orders that all large ships must be destroyed, and that thereafter only small vessels could be built. Besides, he threatened to put to death any Japanese who should return to his country after having been abroad, even if he had been carried away against his will. No foreigner could come to Japan and no Japanese could leave his country. They could, therefore, learn nothing from other people. That is why I said that Japan had been asleep for more than two hundred years.

In all that long time there had been no change. Just as Japan was in 1621, so it was in 1853. The houses were still built in exactly the same way, the men and boys dressed exactly as their ancestors had done before, and so did the women and girls, and they lived in the same manner.

The people worked hard from early in the morning until late at night. The merchants, mechanics, and farmers, toiled from the beginning of the year to the end, without any Sundays or holidays, except on New Year's day, and perhaps a few days later. They had nothing to say in the government, and belonged to the Lord on whose estate they were living. The whole of Japan was divided into about three hundred of such estates; some of them very large and others again very small. Over each of these estates was a daimiyo,[4] or lord, who was assisted by as many samurai,[5] or knights, as the estate could support. These knights were the civil officers of the estate while there was peace; but as soon as war broke out they were soldiers, always ready to go into battle, and to die for their lord.

The greatest of all the daimiyo was the Shogun[3], or Commander-in-chief, who resided in his large castle at Yedo.[6] It was he who made the laws for all the Japanese, and he had so many samurai that not even the greatest daimiyo dared disobey him. But, although he had as much power as any emperor, still he was not the real Emperor of Japan. Many, many years before there was any Shogun, the country had been governed by the ancestors of a man who was living quietly in Kyoto.[7] His house was shaped like a temple, and stood in the most beautiful grounds that can be imagined. When the people spoke of him, they whispered: Tenshi Sama,[8] for he was to them the Child of Heaven, the descendant, as they thought, of the gods who created Japan.

But Tenshi Sama, they believed, was too mighty and too great to care about such a small thing as governing the people. All he had to do was to pray to the gods to take care of Japan, and they would surely hear his prayers. Since the first Shogun ruled over Japan, there had been many wars and much bloodshed, because many daimiyo wanted larger estates than they possessed. All these wars ceased in the year 1600, when the Daimiyo of Tokugawa,[9] named Iyeyasu,[10] defeated his rivals at Sekigahara,[11] and caused the Tenshi Sama to make him Shogun.

"PEACE REIGNED OVER THE COUNTRY."

Iyeyasu was such a brave general, and besides an able as well as a generous man, that the country began to enjoy peace. The great daimiyo tried once more to shake off his rule, but they could not do it. In 1615 the last battle was fought, and the daimiyo were defeated so badly that they gave in. Iyeyasu punished some of them very severely. He took a very large part of the estate of Lord Mori,[12] the Daimiyo of Choshiu,[13] and divided it among two of his sons. Mori henceforth was the enemy of Tokugawa, and so were all the great daimiyo who had suffered defeat. But Iyeyasu ordered them to build yashiki,[14] or mansions, in Yedo, and to live there half of the year. Iyemitsu,[15] the grandson of Iyeyasu and the third Tokugawa Shogun, commanded them to leave their wives and children at Yedo, where he held them in his power. He made laws for the people, the samurai, and the daimiyo, and, since he had an army of 80,000 samurai on his own estates, he was strong enough to make the daimiyo obey him.

Thus all war ceased in Japan and peace reigned over the country. The merchant plied his trade, the mechanic worked at his craft, and the peasant toiled in his field, as their fathers had done before them, and they brought up their sons to do as they had been taught. There was, therefore, no progress; and there was very little liberty.

The only people who really did have something to say, were the samurai or knights. They did not work, but were paid by the daimiyo whom they served. They were very proud of being *gentlemen*, and never failed to speak and act as they believed was right. Thus Japan continued until the year 1853. Then a number of "fire-ships," their smoke stacks belching forth a dense smoke, steamed up Yedo Bay. The cliffs echoed the throbbing of the engines. In vain did the Shogun's guard boats warn them to go back. They did not heed these commands any more than when the tide turned, and the current tried to stop their progress.[A] On, on they went toward the capital of the Shogun, until the shoaling water warned them to cast anchor. Their commander was notified that he must leave, but he replied that he carried a letter for the Shogun, and would not go before he had delivered it. The government at Yedo did not know what to do. The Japanese are very shrewd, and understood quite well that the samurai, armed with bow and arrow and in old fashioned lacquered armor, were no match for guns and cannon. The government was *afraid to refuse* to receive the letter, and a year later it signed a treaty, because *it was afraid* to enter upon war with these strangers. The officers of the government knew the strength of the foreigners, but the samurai of the other daimiyo did not; and when they heard that the Shogun had entered into a treaty, *because he was afraid*, they became angry and excited. From that time it was certain that the Tokugawa princes would be Shogun no longer. The anger of the samurai increased when a new treaty was made, in 1858, between the government of Japan and that of the United States through Mr. Townsend Harris. For the following ten years there was trouble in Japan, and the samurai began to think that Tenshi Sama should drive the foreigners into the ocean. That was easier said than done, but the samurai did succeed in taking the government away from the Tokugawa, and Tenshi Sama became emperor indeed, and he is so still.

Mutsuhito,[16] the Emperor of Japan, was only a boy of fifteen when he was taken out of his beautiful palace in 1867. He is now (1900) forty-eight years old, and has seen Japan grow from a poor little country into a great and strong empire. Our story begins in the year 1858, and will show how a Japanese samurai boy was brought up.

II
THE OLD YASHIKI

GREAT preparations for receiving guests were being made in the Kano Yashiki at Nagato. To-morrow would be the fifth day of the eleventh month of the fourth year of the oldest son and heir, and the boy would be invested with the *hakama*[17] of the samurai.

There would be a great gathering of the Choshiu clan, for the Kano family had been great in the council, and was trusted by daimiyo and samurai alike. The history of the Mori family was as much the history of that of Kano, at least ever since Kano Shimpei had tried to keep his lord from fighting Iyeyasu. The Mori of that time had refused to heed his knight's advice, and sent him away in disgrace. But Kano would not desert his master. He had followed him to Osaka, and when the battle was lost, had saved his lord by continuing to fight until Mori was rescued by a small band of devoted samurai. Kano himself died covered with wounds. The Daimiyo of Choshiu had never forgotten the advice nor the heroic death of Kano Shimpei. They had honored his descendants, and every Kano had tried to show his great loyalty to his lord.

The Kano Yashiki stood within the outer moat of Choshiu's castle. A massive gateway faced the street. On each side was a high, plastered wall covered with tiles. This wall surrounded the yashiki and its grounds, and gave it the shape of a perfect square. The doors of the gate were of heavy wood, plated with iron and studded with huge iron bolts. They swung inward on hinges, but were opened only for the daimiyo, if he should honor his samurai with a visit, or for a knight of equal rank of the owner. For all other callers there was a little gate by the side, where the guard could examine all that entered or left.

A short but broad road, composed of pulverized shells mixed with soft white sand, led from the gate to the samurai residence. It was a fine two story building, with verandahs running round the house. It was built upon posts about two feet high and resting upon stones so that, if an earthquake should happen, the building could move with the wave of the earth. The verandahs were made of kayaki[18] wood, and polished until it shone like a mirror. The building was really a large and strong shed, with thick posts upholding the roof with its heavy tiles. There were no walls. Paper sho ji,[19] or sliding doors, set loosely in grooves, took their place. They could be easily taken out, to allow fresh air. These grooves were so arranged that the whole floor could easily be changed into several apartments or rooms. The upper story had a balcony at the back, overlooking the spacious and beautifully kept gardens, with ponds, little hills, and copses of trees. At the end of the balcony as well as on the verandahs were closets, holding the ame,[20] or rain doors. These were slid into deep grooves along the outer edges of the verandahs and balcony at night or when a storm arose.

The owner of the house was sitting in one of the rooms at the back of the house. He was a man of about thirty, of middle size, but strongly built. His hibachi[21] stood before him, but he was evidently in deep thought. He did not expect any visitors, for he had taken off his hakama, and was sitting in his simple cotton kimono,[22] or gown.

Suddenly he clapped his hands three times. The sound of: hai, hai![23] came from a distance, and presently one of the sho ji was slid aside, and Mrs. Kano appeared dutifully on hands and knees. She could not be seen very well, as she bowed her head upon her hands, as a salute to her master and husband, but when he remained silent, she raised her head and asked softly:[24]

"Did you call?"

She could be seen now. Mrs. Kano was perhaps eighteen, certainly not more than nineteen years old. Her jet black hair was done up in a matronly coil and glistening with patchouli or oil from the cactus plant. Her forehead was fair, but eye-brows she had none, for a Japanese wife, before her marriage, was compelled to pull them out. Her teeth were of a shining jet, another custom of married ladies. But, disfigured as she was, her soft and gentle voice showed that Mrs. Kano had been taught the Onna Daigaku,[25] or the Greater Learning for Women, and that she was willing to try to please her husband.

When he heard his wife's voice, Kano looked at her, bowed slightly, and said:

"Have all preparations been made for to-morrow's reception?"

"Yes," she replied, "all your orders have been obeyed."

"Very well," he said, and she withdrew.

Kano was thinking of his son. He remembered the death of his father, when he was only eighteen years old. How he had looked up to him! How gently, and yet how firmly had his father trained him in the manly exercises of the samurai, hardening his body to despise luxury and ready to bear cold or heat at any time. How he had taught him the family history, with its fine record of loyalty and self sacrifice, and how he had commanded him to follow in the same path. Kano felt that he had done so. He remembered the illness which had struck the strong man so suddenly and with fatal ending, and which caused the son such a deep pain. His father's last words: "The wise man of China says that the greatest disrespect to a father is not to have any son," had caused him to marry as soon as the time of mourning was over. And now he was a father himself, and the time had come that he must begin to train the child.

Had he done his duty, according to the laws and custom of the samurai? Why, certainly. On the seventy-fifth day after its birth, the child had left off its baby-linen. On the hundred and twentieth day it had been weaned. Every ceremony had been observed as it should be by a gentleman of Kano's family. Kano's own brother had fed the child; and My Lord's cousin had acted as sponsor. He had taken the child on his left knee and as weaning father had taken of the sacred rice which had been offered to the gods. He had dipped his chop-sticks three times in it, and then placed them in the mouth of the child as if giving it some of the rice juice. He had followed the honored custom to feed the child three times from the five cakes made of rice meal. When the three cups of sake[26] were brought on the tray, the sponsor drank them and offered one to the child, now restored to his guardian. The boy pretended to drink two cups, and the sponsor had produced his present. Every ceremony had been observed, and the feast which followed had shown that Kano intended to follow in the footsteps of his fathers, in honoring the customs of Old Japan.

Again on the fifteenth day of the eleventh month, when the boy's hair was allowed to grow, not a single ceremony was neglected; and to-morrow Kano would prove once more that he loved the customs of his father and was willing to abide by them.

Again a sho ji slid open, but this time it attracted Kano's attention. A servant girl kneeling on the door sill was waiting until her master should speak.

"What is it?" he asked.

With a deep drawn breath, as if overwhelmed at the honor of being spoken to, she replied:

"Mr. Hattori[27] wishes to speak to your honor."

Kano rose hastily and, opening a cupboard, seized his hakama and slipped it on over his kimono. Thus prepared to receive his old-time friend, he ordered the girl to admit him. A moment later, and the visitor entered with a shuffling gait, and, falling upon his knees, three times touched his head to the ground. Kano replied in the same manner, each in turn repeating the same ceremonious phrases, which custom demanded of men of their rank.

At last Hattori was seated upon the cushion which the servant had placed for him, and tea was brought in. When the servant had withdrawn, the two men smoked in silence, until Hattori knocked the ashes out of his pipe, and asked:

"Have you seen him?"

Kano raised his brows slightly, and answered:

"I do not understand you. Do you mean the sponsor? Certainly, I have seen him."

"Ah! you are thinking of to-morrow! No, I do not mean the sponsor or any one connected with your family. Bah! I mean the new guest we must entertain, and who will offer you his congratulations."

"A new guest!" exclaimed Kano. "Surely, I must be growing dull, for I fail to catch your meaning."

"Well, then," said Hattori, cautiously looking into the garden, "another metsuké[28] arrived this afternoon from Yedo, and was bold enough to come to the castle and demand to be admitted. I was ordered to receive him and find out what he wanted. When I came into the room where he was waiting, he introduced himself by handing me a letter from the Go rojiu,[29] to the clan. There were enough councillors present to open it, so I excused myself and called our friends. It was very brief and to the point. The Go rojiu desires to mention our clan as a model for Japan, and has therefore sent this fellow to report."

"What is his name?"

"Sawa."[30]

"Sawa, Sawa," repeated Kano slowly. "I think I know the name. How old is he, do you think?"

"He must be forty at least, and he seems cut out for his work. His oily talk is disgusting; and while he flatters you, his eyes are restlessly peeping in every nook and corner."

"What have you done with him?"

"The usual thing. We accepted the letter and told him that we would deliberate carefully about it, and let him have an answer in a couple of days. He bowed himself out and was carried in his norimono[31] to the hotel. But I hear he has sent his servants to find out if he can not rent a vacant yashiki. So, you see, he intends to remain some time, and send in a full report."

Kano was silent. He was evidently displeased; suddenly his attention as well as that of his friend was drawn to a soft footstep on the gravel walk of the garden, and presently a young man appeared at the steps leading from the verandah to the path. He faced the room and bowed low. Both returned the salutation, but Kano muttered between his teeth: "Ito![32] What on earth brings him here?"

III
THE MESSENGER

THE intruder, if he may be so called, mounted the steps and, entering the room, saluted in the usual manner. He was invited to approach, and, clapping his hands, Kano ordered the servant to bring in another cushion, and fresh tea. When these had been brought, and the visitor was seated, Kano said:

"When did you leave Yedo?"

"Just a week ago."

"Is there anything new?"

"Why, I think so. It is said openly by Tokugawa men that the foreign devils, with whom the Go rojiu have made a treaty, will be permitted to settle down at Yokohama."

"Settle down! What do you mean?" exclaimed Hattori.

"Where is Yokohama?" asked Kano.

Ito replied first to the question of his host.

"Yokohama is a little distance from the Tokaido,[33] near Kanagawa, the last post station at this side of Yedo." Then, turning toward Hattori, he continued:—"Yes; the new treaty permits them to buy land and to build houses."

"But," said Hattori, aghast, "that means that Japan is invaded. These foreign devils have come with their fire ships and guns, and by threats have accomplished their purpose. What has become of the Tokugawa? Have they lost their manhood, to submit to such a disgrace!"

"Softly!" said Kano. "There may be reasons why the Go rojiu has permitted them to come so close to Yedo. It must be so. It must be a trap to destroy the intruders in such a manner that others like them will think twice before they come again."

"I wish I could think so," said Ito. "No! I believe that the Tokugawa are afraid of an invasion. Their samurai, with the exception of those of Mito and Aidzu,[34] are not worth their salt. Have you ever seen, during your residence in Yedo, a Tokugawa Knight practising at arms. They are quick enough to draw their swords upon a beggar or a merchant, but when they meet one of the samurai of the southern clans, they fly to cover. No! Since Ii Naosuke[35] is regent, he has looked closely into the forces which the Tokugawa can muster, if a war should break out, and he thinks that it must be avoided at any cost. Of course, he expects that the samurai of the great clans will be furious, and he has sent a large number of spies to report what is said. One of these gentry was sent here. I heard of it in time to follow him, and I came on to warn you."

Both Kano and Hattori expressed their thanks, and Kano said:

"But if the Tokugawa are not able to prevent a handful of foreigners from landing, how can they expect that the great southern clans will obey them?"

"Oh!" replied Ito, smiling grimly; "we have been obedient for so many years, trembling when the Go rojiu frowned, that the regent believes it will continue forever. He had a meeting of all the daimiyo connected with his clan, and tried to convince them that we must now receive these foreigners, and try to learn all that they know. Then, when we can handle their fire ships and their cannon, we may expect to drive them into the sea."

A JAPANESE FAMILY.

Hattori put his hand upon his dagger, but Kano, with a friendly motion of his hand, calmed him. "There may be something in that," he said thoughtfully. "Mind you!" he continued, "I do not underrate Japanese courage, but we do not know the strength of these barbarians. We have been living like frogs in a well. It is easy enough to engage in war, but it is best to know the number of the enemy, before you engage in what may prove too heavy odds. Such a thing would be foolish. But we may come to a settlement with the Tokugawa. If indeed, their samurai have lost their courage, then my lord of Choshiu may recover the land from which he was robbed, and I may avenge my ancestor's death. When will the councillors of the clan meet?"

"The day after to-morrow," replied Hattori.

Kano clapped his hands, and ordered the servant to send up dinner for his guests and himself. Hattori and Ito made some excuses, but were easily induced to remain.

Small tables were brought in and placed before each man. First sake or wine made from rice, was served hot, and a small stone bottle placed near each person; then there was *suimono*, a sort of vegetable soup, after which rice was ladled out into cups or bowls. A number of side dishes, such as pickled *daikon*, a sort of giant radish, *tsubo* or stewed sea-weed, and soy, a sauce, were enjoyed by the samurai.

The conversation had been interrupted when the servants entered, and was not resumed. The men spoke of the ceremony to take place the next day; and Ito was invited. Before leaving, however, Kano told Hattori that he would ask the councillors of the clan to remain after the reception was over, so that they might discuss their plans for the future.

Ito and Hattori bowed good-bye, as they were going in different directions. Each carried a lantern, for it was dark, and there was no street lighting in Japan at that time. At the corner of the street, Ito stopped as if in doubt. Then, after a few moments, he seemed to make up his mind, for he turned to the left, and went hastily toward the castle entrance. The heavy gate was closed, but the little side gate stood ajar. Ito entered, and giving his name to the officer of the guard, went along the barracks where many of the samurai of lower rank dwelt. At last he stopped before a small door, and knocked softly. He heard a shuffling of feet, and a woman's voice demanded who was there.

"Is Mr. Inouye[36] in?" he asked.

"Yes."

"Tell him that Ito Saburo wishes to see him."

The woman seemed satisfied, for the door slid open, and Ito entered. Without waiting he mounted the steps, and opening a sho ji, stepped into a room, dimly lit by a rushlight placed in a paper lantern. Ito fell on his knees, and saluted in the usual manner, which salute was returned by the owner of the room, a man of Ito's age, but of more slender build.

The two men had not met for two years; for Ito had been ordered to remain at the Choshiu yashiki in Yedo, and Inouye's duties had kept him at Nagato. But they had corresponded by every courier carrying letters to and from the capital, for they had been friends ever since they were little boys. Yet when they met after such a long absence, there was no glad "Helloh!" with a hearty clasp of the hand, as we would meet an old friend. Pleased as they were to see each other again, they had been taught that good breeding demands that gentlemen should always show courtesy and respect to others of their own rank. Certain sentences must be uttered before any ordinary conversation can begin. Therefore Ito said:

"I was very rude the last time we met, but I hope you have forgiven me."

"No," replied Inouye, "it was I who was rude, and I pray you to overlook it."

It is needless to say that neither of them had really been rude, but custom demanded that this should be said, and the same custom prevails in Japan to-day. We think that it is foolish, and the Japanese think us very rude, because we do not obey that custom.

After these customs had been observed, the two friends sat down, and Ito said:

"Has any progress been made in your studies of the barbarian nations?"

"Nothing worth boasting. I have been twice to Nagasaki to try if I could pick up some of the books of the Hollanders, but the Tokugawa officers will not permit any stranger to approach the island of Deshima, unless they are bribed with more money than I possess. Still, I have learned enough to know that Japan is not in a condition to fight the barbarians, and I am afraid, I think, that the regent was right in submitting to their demands."

"I do not think so," replied Ito. "Right! What right has the Tokuwaga to sell an inch of Japan's soil. It does not belong to them. It is the property of Tenshi Sama, if it belongs to anybody. It makes me angry to think that we can no longer boast that

> The foot of the invader has never trod our soil."

"There will be no invasion," said Inouye. "These men only want to trade. If they had intended to use force, they would have done so when they came the second time, with a large fleet. No! I do not believe that our country is in danger, at least not for some years. But they may come as spies to find out what opportunity there is to obtain possession of Japan. The Yedo government should try to discover what the intentions of the barbarians really are."

"The Yedo government is only anxious to make money. You do not know, Inouye, how good it feels to breathe the pure air of Nagato. It is stifling at Yedo. Spies, spies are everywhere. The Tokugawa samurai seem to have forgotten that they are gentlemen, and how a samurai should behave. They are quick enough to draw their swords upon men who cannot defend themselves, but they are nimble with their feet when hard blows may be expected. If Japan must go to war, we, the samurai of the south will do the fighting. The day of the Tokuwaga is past."

There was a brief silence, when Inouye said:

"I have not yet asked you what brings you here. I had not heard that you had been relieved from duty at Yedo."

"I was not relieved. But we were informed that the Go rojiu intended to send new spies to the southern diamiyo, and I was ordered to inform the councillors of the clan. It seems that Sawa, the chief spy, arrived just before me. I suppose I shall be told to return to Yedo, but I hope not. At any rate I shall see you before I leave."

After the usual salutations Ito rose and lit his candle. After leaving the door, he went through the grounds to the opposite barracks, where his mother lived. Knocking at the little wicket, he was admitted with many bows and glad exclamations. These he returned with some pleasant words, and entered the sitting-room. Presently his mother entered, and both knelt down and saluted in the respectful and courteous manner of their people. There was no kissing or even handshaking; both were, of course, very happy, but Japanese law forbade showing joy, even in the expression of the face. Ito would have obeyed at once any order his mother might have given him; but she considered him as the head of the family, and showed that she looked upon him as the master of the house.

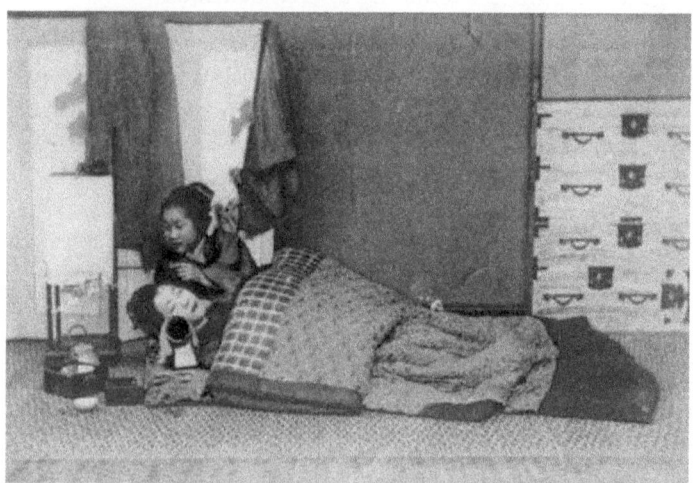

"HIS MOTHER, SUFFERING FROM RHEUMATISM, TO RECEIVE MASSAGE TREATMENT FROM ONE OF THE SERVANTS."

They chatted for half an hour about their acquaintances and then retired. Ito's mother, suffering from rheumatism, to receive a massage treatment from one of the servants.

IV
THE FIFTH DAY OF THE ELEVENTH MONTH

THE day broke calm and smiling. Japan, especially those parts around the Inland Sea, has a lovely climate. It is seldom that the sky is not of a deep blue color, and the days are few when children cannot play or walk in the streets. They are rarely kept in the house. Young babies are securely fastened upon the backs of children six or seven years old, and sent into the streets. There are no noisy games. Girls play sometimes battledore and shuttlecock, but the boys are too dignified. American boys would be surprised if they saw two Japanese school friends meet in the street. They do not approach with a hop, skip and jump, or clap each other on the shoulder. Oh no! They stop as soon as they meet, take off their caps, for all Japanese schoolboys wear now a sort of soldier cap, and then bow almost to the ground. Then they draw a deep breath, and each continues on his way.

The great difference between Japanese and American boys of the same age, is that all our boys are fond of fun, and we are glad to see them have a good time, while a Japanese boy would not be able to understand what we call fun. Our boys would soon grow sick if there were not some time in the day when they could make all the noise they wished. If a Japanese boy should make even the slightest unnecessary noise at home, his parents would think that the world had turned topsy-turvy. From his earliest youth, the boy is trained not to show his feelings. In all the years of my life in Japan, I have never seen a boy of over six years old with tears in his eyes.

It is eleven o'clock, and the guests begin to arrive. They come mostly on foot, for they all live in the neighborhood; but there are a few who hold such a high rank that they can only leave their yashiki in a sedan chair, or on horseback. A servant brings a large bundle, carefully wrapped. It is taken to the back room which has been made much larger by the removal of several sho ji. Here Mr. Kano sits in hakama and *haori*,[37] receiving each guest as he enters according to his rank in the clan. To some his bows are deeper and more prolonged, with others they are more simple, although at the entrance of every guest, his forehead touches his hands, spread out upon the floor before him. The visitors take their places about the room in the order of their rank, each saluting the host as he enters and thereafter the guests. Waitresses in a kneeling posture serve tea. At last a man of dignified bearing, clothed in rich silk, enters, and after saluting, sits down upon a cushion prepared for him near the master of the house. Kano is about to clap his hands, as a signal for his son to be brought in, when a man-servant opens a sho ji, and kneeling with his head almost touching the mats, crawls toward his master. He whispers:

"Mr. Sawa of Yedo desires to present his respects."

Kano slightly raises his eyebrows, but by a slight bending forward indicates that the new-comer shall be admitted. After a few moments the latest guest enters and prostrates himself before his host, who returns the compliment. Kano with a slight motion of the arm indicates the place which he intends him to occupy, and Sawa, crouching and bowing to the guests proceeds in that direction. It is between the seats of the councillors and those of the chief samurai, and, as it happens, next to that of Ito.

Not a single glance showed that the visitor was unwelcome. No expression of approval had escaped their lips upon the entrance of a popular member of the clan, and not a sign showed that Sawa's appearance at this time was resented. They sat unmoved, like the North American Indian chiefs. Kano clapped his hands, and the servant brought in a board, resembling one of our checkerboards; it was placed upon the mat near the father, facing the point of the compass which had been declared lucky by a fortune teller. The gentleman at Kano's side then clapped his hands, and another servant brought in the package which had been delivered before. It was unwrapped, and contained a Kimono of fine silk, with beautifully embroidered storks and tortoises, fir trees and bamboos. This was as it should be. Storks and tortoises promised long life to the boy; for the Japanese believed that the stork lives a thousand years, and the tortoise ten thousand. The fir tree never changes its color, therefore the child will possess an unchanging virtuous heart, and the bamboo, as it shoots up straight, will give him an upright mind.

The servant holds up the dress for the inspection of the guests, who, after looking at it, express their approval by bowing low, and a deep drawn sigh. Presently Mrs. Kano, who has been watching the ceremony from a near apartment through a convenient slit in the sho ji, enters leading the boy. Both kneel at the entrance and after touching the ground three times with the forehead, the child is brought to his father, who places him upon the checkerboard facing the east, because that is the lucky point. The mother dresses him in the Kimono presented by the sponsor, and puts on the hakama; then the child receives an imitation sword and dirk, which are placed in his sash. Then sake is brought in and the sponsor and child exchange cups. This ends the ceremony which admits the three-year-old boy among the samurai of the clan.

Mother and son, after repeating their salutations, leave the room and refreshments are served. Gradually the sense of ceremony disappears, and conversation becomes more general. Kano, apparently deeply engaged in talking with the sponsor, keeps a watchful eye over his guests, and frequently casts a glance toward the spot occupied by Sawa. The sponsor, an elderly gentleman of dignified bearing, at last notices his host's looks, and says:

"Who is that gentleman? He is a stranger to me, and I cannot distinguish his coat of arms."

"He bears the Tokugawa crest, your lordship," replies Kano, "and is the new O Metsuke, whom the Council at Yedo have kindly sent to report upon our model clan."

The old gentleman did not notice the sarcasm. "When did he arrive, and why was his arrival not made known to me?" he inquired in a slightly offended tone. Kano bowed, and replied:

"Mr. Sawa arrived yesterday afternoon, and presented his letter at the castle, where Councillor Hattori was ordered to receive him. As we had not been notified by the Go rojiu of their intention to send us a metsuké, Mr. Hattori thought that the letter should be submitted to the council of the clan. I have noticed that he has spoken to the councillors, who will wait here until the other guests have withdrawn. If it please your lordship, we shall be glad to have the benefit of your advice."

"No, I cannot spare the time, and the matter is of no great importance," declared his lordship, continuing his repast. Presently they were joined by Hattori, for whom a cushion was brought, and who, after the prescribed bows of respect, took no further notice of Mori's cousin.

"I think, friend Kano," he said, "that you may as well keep an eye upon your honored guest, Mr. Sawa. The fellow seems to think that he is at Yedo, instead of in a gentleman's yashiki and that he can do as he pleases. He has filled his sake cup quite often, and has been offensive, to judge by the looks of Ito."

"I have perceived it," replied Kano, "but Ito will, I am sure, keep his temper, and settle with the intruder upon a more favorable occasion. I am more afraid of the young fellows who seem to have heard some insulting remarks. Pray, entertain his lordship, while I dismiss the guests." Without waiting for a reply, Kano rose and, bowing before each guest, advanced toward Sawa. There he knelt down and performed the usual salutations somewhat stiffly. Sawa returned them as well as he could.

When they had regained their upright positions, Kano addressed his self-invited guest, and said in a tone loud enough for some young samurai close by to hear:

"I am deeply grateful to the Go rojiu for remembering me on this occasion. I do not know how I deserved this honor."

Sawa had some difficulty to hide a grin. Did this country bumpkin really fancy that the great Council of the Tokugawa cared anything about him or his family. Amused at the thought, he bowed, and said:

"The Go rojiu no doubt, if it had only known of the event, would have been glad to honor his host upon this occasion. It was known," he added more soberly and looking sharply at Kano, "that the Choshiu clan was directed almost entirely by the wisdom of his entertainer, and the question had been discussed to secure his services for the Council. Unfortunately the law of Iyeyasu forbade it. Only members of the Tokugawa clan were permitted to serve the Shogun. But this did not prevent the Council from profiting by the wisdom of Kano the Councillor, and it was to secure this benefit that he, Sawa, had been directed to reside in the clan."

Kano bowed, and replied. "It is a very great honor, indeed, and, no doubt, well deserved by such an able man as my guest. Pray, make yourself at home in the clan. You will find every Choshiu gentleman glad to receive a samurai from the capital, where he has advantages to learn manners which we in the country do not possess. But every samurai is glad to excel in chivalry, and we of Choshiu no less than those of other clans."

Again they bowed, and Sawa resumed:

"I understand that this joyful event will be followed by a meeting of the Honorable Council?"

"The regular meeting is to-morrow," replied Kano. "I have received no notice of any extra meeting, nor have I sent out any. It seems to me that you are misinformed."

"Forgive me, my host. Who is that young man, who happened to be my neighbor during the most interesting ceremony? I fancy that I have seen him at Yedo."

"That is probably so. Indeed, it may have been very recently, for he arrived yesterday. Choshiu's yashiki seems to have suffered severely from the last earthquake, and expensive repairs are necessary. Our officer in charge thought it necessary to send a special messenger, but why he did not commission an older man, is beyond my comprehension."

Sawa began to perceive that this country bumpkin was quite able to parry his thrusts; he did not want to give offense, and besides began to feel sleepy. He therefore informed his host of his intention to return to his inn. Kano raised no objection, and after the usual leave taking, escorted his guest to the door, and saw him leave the gate. Calling a young samurai, he bade him see that Sawa did not return to the yashiki, whereupon he re-entered the room. The other guests, seeing that the councillors lingered, withdrew all except Ito, who was asked to wait as he might be wanted.

V
THE COUNCIL OF THE CLAN

BEFORE he seated himself, Kano called his chief samurai, and told him to have the sho ji put in so as to make the apartment of the usual size. He also ordered him to have several men patrol the garden, and to see that no one could approach the house, while he himself was to move noiselessly through the adjoining rooms, and answer for it that there should be no listener. Knowing that his orders would be obeyed, he sat down, ordered tea and hibachi to be brought, and without further ceremony opened the meeting.

"Honorable Councillors," he said, "two messengers have come from Yedo. You have, no doubt, noticed them, for both were here during the ceremony in my humble house. The first one is the new metsuke, Sawa, whom it has pleased the Go rojiu to appoint to our clan. When Mr. Hattori informed me of his arrival, I could not understand the cause of his appointment. Our clan has had no trouble with the Tokugawa for many years; and, although there can be no friendship between the house of Iyeyasu and that of Mori, there has been no open hostility.

"The arrival of the second messenger explains the situation. The Go rojiu has entered into a new treaty with the barbarians, and permitted them to dwell at Yokohama, near Kanagawa on the Tokaido. This fine piece of news is discussed openly at Yedo, and there is no doubt of its truth. The Regent, naturally I think, feels somewhat anxious as to how the great clans will receive it, and has probably sent metsuke to other model clans besides Choshiu. The news is so important that our friend Hattori agreed with me to ask you to discuss it here privately, so that we may decide upon the policy of our clan. Honorable Mr. OKubo, what is your opinion?"

The person thus addressed was the oldest of the councillors, a man grown gray in the service of his clan. He was silent for some moments, gravely sipping his tea. Then he said:

"These questions are not for me to answer. I am only acquainted with Old Japan, as it has existed for hundreds of years, and I am afraid the arrival of these barbarians is a menace to our country. I don't know them, and do not wish to know them; but I do know that, before the Tokugawa were thought of, the barbarians came, and were received kindly by the children of the gods. What was their gratitude? They began to teach a cult which destroyed the relations between parent and child, master and servant, lord and retainer. They were finally expelled, but it cost years of strife, and myriads of lives before their teaching was rooted out of the country. Since then order has been restored, and we have had peace. Now the barbarians will be admitted again, and fresh troubles will commence. Younger and stronger heads than mine will be needed to save our clan and the house of Mori, although, if it comes to war, I shall claim the honor of dying fighting for our lord."

All bowed but protested that OKubo was strong and able enough to lead the councils of the clan; but he replied that his time of usefulness was past, and Kano, out of respect for his wish, addressed the councillor next in years. That gentleman did not see any danger to the clan. Yokohama was a long distance from Nagato, and if there was to be trouble with the barbarians, the Tokugawa would be the first sufferers, for it was within the territory belonging to the Shogun. As to the metsuke, why, they must do as they had done before with such fellows, surround him with spies of their own.

Thus every councillor spoke in turn, the opinion of each being received with grave courtesy. A little more interest was shown when Hattori began to speak. It was known that he was in Kano's confidence, and it was a standing joke that Kano's advice was always adopted.

"Honorable Councillors," said Hattori, bowing deeply, "it ill becomes a man of my age to dispute the opinions of the leaders who for many years have guided the policy of our clan with brilliant success. If I venture to differ with them, it may be from lack of wisdom and experience, but I shall be glad if I am corrected. It is only by the kind teaching of such men as the honorable councillors, that men of my age can be prepared to follow in their footsteps.

"I am afraid that the coming of the barbarians promises evil days, not only for the Tokugawa, but for all the clans. You, gentlemen, remember, how the arrival of the fireships and the signing of the first treaty was followed by incessant earthquakes,[B] how the ocean rose in its fury, and overwhelmed the barbarian ship, supposed to be safely at anchor at Shimoda.[C] Surely, gentlemen, the gods of Japan themselves fought for our country. But the Go rojiu was blind. Was not the Shogun Iyeyoshi himself killed for not defying the barbarians by expelling them? 'We are not strong enough,' says the Regent. There was a time when the countless hosts of Kublai Khan, the conqueror of the world, were hurled upon our shores. What became of them? Tenshi Sama prayed to his ancestors and they, the gods of our country, destroyed the invader. We have nothing to fear, except our own faint-heartedness. Are we, the samurai of Japan, unworthy of our ancestors? Have our muscles grown weak that we can no longer wield the sword? Out upon us, then, for cowards! If the Tokugawa be a coward, out upon the Tokugawa. Choshiu, Kaga, Satsuma, and Tosa, ought to be able to dispose of the foreigners and at the same time of the Tokugawa brood. Let us send confidential messengers to those clans, and, after we have arranged with them, send Mr. Sawa back to Yedo, securely packed in a box labelled: This side up; handle with care!"

A smile of approbation passed through the assembly; only Kano's face showed no sign. It was now his turn to speak, and, after toying with his fan, as if collecting his thoughts, he began:

"Honorable Councillors, I agree with the last speaker that the arrival of the foreigners bodes evil for our country. I do not believe that they will try to make war upon us, unless indeed, we provoke it ourselves. At the present time, at any rate, we are not in a condition to provoke a quarrel. For the past two hundred years the world has moved, and we have stood still; that is why we are helpless. We have found out something. These barbarians possess ships which go wherever they want them, without regard to tide and wind. We must have such ships and learn how to handle them. We, sons of Japan, are not naturally brainless; we can learn what the barbarians have learned, and by hard work, we may be able to surpass them. There may be some trouble with the Tokugawa, but I do not think so, unless they send us another metsuke besides Mr. Sawa. I have taken the measure of that gentleman, and do not think that it would take much gold to make him deaf and blind. But we need not take him into our confidence. We should send a trusty messenger to Nagasaki, and at whatever cost buy some of the books of the Hollanders. Surely, some merchants will be found there who understand that language and teach us. Besides, we must repair our forts, and buy new cannon. Our samurai must practice with their arms during every moment of leisure. Then, gentlemen, when the time comes, we shall be prepared, be it to avenge Sekigahara and the Castle of Osaka, or to drive the barbarian into the sea. My honored ancestor gave the same advice to our illustrious lord's forefather. Oh! that it had been accepted. Mori looks now upon Kii and Owari,[38] and grinds his teeth at the thought that their people, once his property, are now arraigned among his foes. Kano's arm and muscle are as ready for the fray, as those of the youngest warrior, and he will not be the last to unsheath his sword, nor the first to return it to its scabbard. Self-restraint is often much more difficult than exposure to danger.

"The advice of Mr. Hattori supposes that the councillors of Kaga, Satsuma, and Tosa are of our opinion. But we have a feud with Satsuma, who might seize such an opportunity to bring all the power of the Tokugawa down upon us. It is said, and I believe it from what I have seen at Yedo, that the samurai of the Shogun have lost their courage. But what of Mito, Aidzu, Kii, Owari, and the host of other daimiyo ready to march at the Go rojiu's bidding. Gentlemen, an excuse for the Tokugawa to fall upon us *at this time*, would mean ruin for our clan. We cannot even entertain the thought. But we must watch for our opportunity, and when it comes we must be prepared to strike. At present, let it be understood that Mr. Sawa must be perfectly safe in whatever part of Choshiu's domain, but let him be followed, and let his every step be dogged. Every word he utters, even in his sleep, and every syllable he writes must be known to us. Mr. Hattori, will you please, see to it that this is done."

The council agreed with Kano, as it had always done; and it was decided that a sum of money should be placed at Kano's disposal to procure the necessary books and a teacher at Nagasaki. These resolutions were drawn up, and sent to the adviser of the daimiyo to be sealed, after which they became a law.

And the daimiyo? Oh! he was a *Great Name* only. He never interfered with the affairs of the clan, and did not know anything about them. It was the same with the Shogun at Yedo. His seal was used, and laws were made of which he had never heard; and so it was with Tenshi Sama at Kyoto. All these men, Daimiyo, Shogun, and Tenshi Sama were considered as gods, and nobody but their highest servants were ever allowed to look upon them. If any of them was compelled to travel, they were placed in a norimono, with close blinds, and men ran ahead crying: Shita ni iru![39] Down on your knees. Very few people knew the names of the councillors who did rule in Japan, but the names of those who did not rule, were generally known.

VI
YOUNG KANO GROWS UP

WHILE the Choshiu clan as well as the other clans of Japan, were anxiously watching the opening of Japan and the events which follow, Young Kano or Kano Ekichi[40] was taken gradually out of his mother's hands and given to a faithful attendant of his father to be educated as a true samurai should be. Japanese boys are not baptized for there are few Japanese Christians, and in those days there were none; they have, therefore, no baptismal name. They have, however, given names, which are placed behind the family name instead of before it as we do. They would say, for instance, instead of Henry Jones, Jones Henry; they do the same with the words Mister, Master, Mistress or Miss, for all of which they have only one expression: San. If we should speak to master Ekichi Kano, we should say Kano Ekichi San. These given names can be changed without any difficulty. Sometimes the parents change them, at other times the owner of the name changes it himself, and again the Emperor or Tenshi Sama gives an officer a new name. But in that case, it is sure that the owner will keep it so long as he lives.

I can't say that Ekichi had a very pleasant time of it, although, of course, his father and mother loved him. Only they did not show it, as our parents do. As a little baby he was made to rest upon his knees, so that they might grow flexible, for the Japanese do not sit upon chairs, but squat upon their mats. When he rose in the morning from his futon[41] or comforter which served him as a bed, there was no running to his father or mother, shouting good morning, and giving them a hug or a hearty kiss. When he did meet them, the first thing was to fall on his knees, spread his hands flat before him, and bow until his head rested upon the back of his hands. His father and mother gravely returned the salutation in the same manner. When he took his meals, he was not permitted to say a word. He ate what was put before him, and it was every day the same. Asa meshi, hiru meshi, and ban meshi, or in English, morning rice, noon rice, and evening rice, there was no difference between breakfast, dinner, and supper. Until he was six years old, Ekichi spent most of his time with his attendant in the garden. They strolled around, and he asked questions which the man answered as well as he could. He was taught how to speak to a superior, to an equal, and to an inferior; how long he must remain prostrate before a daimiyo, before a councillor, and before a simple samurai. He was also taken to the grave of his grandfather, and told to kneel down and say his prayers. That was something he could not understand, and which his attendant could not explain; when he asked him, and he did often, the man would say: "It is so, but you should not ask why, because the gods only know." So, when Ekichi was tired and sat down on the sward, he would often think: What is the use of praying at the grave of a dead man. But he was careful not to express his thoughts to anybody.

He was trained not to show pain, distress, or grief. Whatever happened to him, his face must not betray it. Being constantly in the open air, he grew up healthy and strong, and when he was six years old, he was taken to a school for samurai boys.

Ekichi had been with his attendant beyond the gates of his yashiki, but after the first day, he was told to go and return by himself. He met his schoolfellows with the courtesy which he had been taught so carefully, and was treated by them in the same way. There was no playground. Indeed, I do not believe that any of those boys knew what the word "play" means. Many times, thirty years ago, I have seen samurai boys from eight to sixteen years old, during recess or after schooltime retire to their rooms to smoke their tiny pipes and carry on a quiet conversation; but I never saw them play. The government of Japan has found out that baseball, football, and cricket, are healthy games, and is encouraging these boys to indulge in them. But at that time, a samurai lad would have felt hurt at the thought that he could do such a thing as play.

"IT IS REALLY A DAY DEVOTED TO HACHIMAN, THE GOD OF WAR."

All Japanese boys are very quiet; they are brought up that way; but for the children of the people certain holidays are set apart. The fifth of May, or the fifth day of the fifth month is the boys' festival. It is really a day devoted to Hachiman, the god of war, but it is also called the Feast of Flags. A tall bamboo is erected near every house where a boy was born; for every son a fish, properly shaped and a very good imitation made of air-tight sacks is fastened, with its mouth wide open by means of bamboo hoops. The air enters and, besides inflating the body, causes it to squirm, flap, and dart, about the bamboo. They have other days, but the samurai boys do not observe them. There is still a wide distance between them and the children of the people.

At the time when Ekichi Kano went to school, the children squatted upon the mats, and learned the Japanese syllabary,—for there is no alphabet in Japan,—each vowel is connected with a consonant, and thus forms a syllable. The vowels are the same as with us:

a, i, u, e, o,
pron. ah, ee, oo, ay, oh,
and combined with the consonants
ka, ki, ku, ke, ko,
na, ni, nu, ne, no, etc.

Ekichi, like almost all Japanese boys of his class, learned very quickly, nor did the very difficult Chinese characters frighten him. Long before a Chinese boy could have mastered one-half of them, Ekichi could read and understand a book without much difficulty.

He was now growing used to the restraint which was imposed upon him. He began to understand that the word *pleasure* can have no meaning for a Japanese boy, and then he was made to learn that a boy is better without comforts than with them, except when he is sick. He was taught that there can be and must be but one motive for every action, and that motive must be: duty. Ekichi was but a child, and small for his age; but no boy twice as old in America or Europe, could have shown an equal degree of self-control, and contempt of pain and death with this child.

Japan's laws were cruel, at this time, and most offenses were punished with death. The criminal was made to kneel down, a flash of the sharp sword, a blow, and the head lay severed from the body. Young as he was, Ekichi was often taken to these executions, to accustom him to the sight of blood. His face was closely watched to see if he showed any emotion, and when he came home from these disagreeable sights, he found his rice of the color of blood, for it had been colored on purpose with the juice of salted plums. He was expected to eat heartily of this dish, and, like other samurai boys, did so without the nauseous feelings which our boys would experience under the circumstances. Sometimes, at midnight, he was roused from a sound slumber, and ordered to go to the execution ground, and bring a head. There was no refusal possible. Whatever he might think privately of such an errand, there was but one answer possible, a responsive hai! "yes," and immediate obedience. Thus Ekichi, as all other Japanese boys of his class, was indifferent to heat or cold, and forgot that there was such a thing as "fear." He was not quite twelve, when he was given two real swords, sharp, keen blades, made for use and not for show. He was taught that "the sword is the soul of the samurai," or, in the words of the law as it then prevailed in Japan[42]: "The girded sword is the living soul of the samurai. In the case of a samurai forgetting his sword, act as is appointed: it may not be forgiven."

The child never considered his swords as toys; to him they were objects of reverence; that little dirk, eight inches long, might at some time be used to end his own life. He learned how he should behave and act, if ever such a moment should come. There is an instance in Japanese history, when a samurai boy only seven years old, committed suicide that he might save his father. Such stories were told him constantly, and roused his enthusiasm. At no time, after he was twelve years old, would Ekichi have hesitated to take his own life, if he had thought it his duty.

At this age he divided his time between shooting with bow and arrow, riding, fencing and wrestling, and the study of Chinese. He learned to swim and to handle a boat, and as he grew stronger, all dainties and comforts were taken away. If, in winter, his hands became numb, he was told to rub them in snow or water to make them warm; but he was not allowed the use of a fire. The duty of implicit obedience had been planted in him. No Japanese boy would think of asking why? when ordered to do something. Last of all he became master of that exceeding courtesy, peculiar to Japanese gentlemen, and which we foreigners cannot appreciate.

VII
KANO'S JOURNEY TO YEDO

THE 1st of July, 1859, had come and gone, and the barbarians had been admitted into the Country of the Gods. They were only a handful; so few that Choshiu's samurai could have pushed them into the bay by sheer force of numbers. While the Japanese people continued to toil, and cared nothing if there were any barbarians in the country or not, the samurai were getting more and more angry. Still, there was much curiosity mixed with this anger. The barbarians were so few in number; how could the Tokugawa, able to call an army of 80,000 men under arms, be afraid of them.

That puzzled Choshiu's councillors. They had not succeeded in their attempts to obtain books and a teacher at Nagasaki, and it had been decided that another effort should be made at Yokohama. This time the enterprise was thought so important, that it was determined to send one of the councillors, and the choice fell upon Kano. He accepted the commission.

When the councillors separated, Kano requested his friend Hattori to call that evening, as he wished to consult him. Hattori agreed to do so, and punctually to the time appeared at the Kano yashiki.

When the two friends were seated, Kano said, "I have been thinking how I shall go. At first I thought of asking a Go rojiu passport through our *honest* friend Sawa, who will do anything we ask of him, as soon as he sees our gold. But I am afraid it will not do. The Go rojiu must, by this time, have grown suspicious at the excellent reports furnished by their metsuke, and I should certainly be shadowed as soon as they heard that one of Choshiu's councillors was visiting the Kwantô.[43] With spies constantly at my heels, I could not do anything; therefore, nobody except you, must know of my absence. I must, of course, trust my household, but I know that I can do that, I have decided to fall suddenly ill and call for a physician who will tell me that it is a slow fever. So I shall not want him again, since he cannot cure me anyhow. You must call two or three times a week, and spread the report that I am neither better nor worse. If our fellow-councillors ask for me, tell them that I intend to start at an early day."

"But how will you pass the barriers on the Tokaido and the Nakasendo[44]?"

"I shall probably go by sea from Hyogo. I know that this journey is one of danger, but I must not risk the clan. I have, therefore, written to My Lord that I am no longer one of his samurai, but a *rônin*.[45] You must keep this paper and deliver it to the Council only in case I am arrested."

Hattori bowed in assent, took the paper and hid it within the folds of his kimono. He then asked: "Are you going alone?"

"No. I must take a trusty young fellow with me, if something should happen to me. First I thought of Ito, but he is in Tokyo, and may be watched. I have sent for his friend Inouye, who, I am sure, has his wits about him."

"I hardly think that a man like Inouye, who is more given to studying than to tramping about, will like such an adventure," said Hattori, smiling. "But if he consents, you could have no better man."

"That is what I thought. He has, moreover, this advantage, that he can not be known to any Tokugawa officer, since he has never been at Yedo."

"When will you leave?"

"The sooner the better, to-night, if I can induce my intended companion to leave his books so soon. Ah! here he is!"

A servant had announced the visitor by opening a sho ji, and permitting him to enter. The customary salutations passed, and Inouye was requested to join the two friends. Kano scanned him closely, and, evidently pleased with the result, said:

"Mr. Inouye, you can serve the clan; are you willing to do so, even though it involves considerable danger?"

"With all my heart," replied Inouye simply.

"Thank you, in name of the clan. How long will it take you to get ready for a long journey?"

"I can go now."

Both Kano and Hattori smiled with pleasure at the young man's brief replies, and the former explained his scheme in all its bearings. When he had finished Inouye said:

"I thank you, Mr. Councillor, very much for having thought me worthy of this honor, and I shall try not to disappoint you. If you permit me, I shall now write a similar letter to My Lord Mori, and perhaps Mr. Hattori will do me the favor to keep it with that of your honor."

Hattori bowed, and Kano, begging to be excused, withdrew while Inouye was writing his letter. Kano went directly to the room where his wife was. He entered, and, without forgetting to pay her due respects, he said:

"I am leaving on a long journey, but I want people to think that I am ill. I shall, therefore, lie down, and do you send for a physician. Before he comes, send for Mr. Fujii,[46] I shall tell him what to do in my absence."

Kano's instructions were followed. The physician went home very proud at having discovered at once the councillor's sickness. He was sorry that he had been dismissed, but felt that Kano was right. All his medicines could not cure such a fever. And when he thought of the fee in his pocket, his heart almost leaped for joy. It was more than he had received in six months.

The following morning, long before sunrise and while everybody in the Yashiki was fast asleep, Mr. Fujii cautiously opened the little gate, and two samurai, with their faces half hidden in a cloth wrapped around their heads, stepped briskly out. They wore straw sandals, so that their footsteps were inaudible. Fujii bowed deeply, and received a parting bow in return, but not a word was spoken. After passing across the moat, they came to the great highway and turned eastward. When the sun rose they had covered ten miles, and decided to stop for breakfast at the first yadoya[47] they should see.

After six days' traveling without meeting any adventure, although they had met several ruffian-looking rônin, they approached Hyogo. They had carefully discussed their plans and decided to take passage in some trading junk, bound for Yedo or Kanagawa. If they could not do so, they would hire a boat. Kano had been many times along this road, in charge of Mori's procession, and knew Hyogo well. But as he knew that passports were demanded from every traveler stopping at an inn, they decided to pass the night at a village yadoya, and proceed to Hyogo on the following morning.

They found what they wanted two miles west of Hyogo. After securing their rooms, they had their bath, and ordered dinner. Presently they heard the shrill voice of the landlady scolding somebody roundly.

"You little lout" (hyakusho[48]), she shouted, "I sent you for fresh fish, and you come back to tell me that there was none. No fresh fish in Hyogo! Just think of it! And here are two honorable gentlemen, who have ordered their supper! You shall go right back, you blockhead, and bring me fish, fresh fish, do you hear?"

Kano was amused, but Inouye whispered to him, "Suppose we ask that little hyakusho to find out if there is any ship sailing for Yedo. Those little fellows who look so stupid, are often keen enough, if they know that there is some cash for them. Shall I see him?"

Kano nodded assent, and Inouye descended to the ground floor. The boy, a strong built lad of fifteen or sixteen, was receiving the last instructions, and Inouye strolled slowly on the road toward Hyogo. He had not gone a hundred yards, when he heard steps behind him, and turning round saw the boy coming at a great pace. As the boy was about to pass him, Inouye said:

"Wait a moment."

The boy stopped and bowed. Inouye continued:

"You are going to Hyogo, are you not?"

The boy bowed again and muttered:—"I am, your honor."

"Very well. My brother and myself are stopping at yonder hotel. We have had a long march and are tired, but we must go to Yedo as soon as we can. Can you find out if any ships are leaving, and if they take any passengers? You are a sharp boy, and can find out if you try. If you do your errand well, slip up-stairs so that the landlady does not see it, and I shall pay you well."

The boy looked up when he heard himself called a sharp boy, and Inouye felt that he had struck the right chord. He returned to the yadoya, where he found Kano fast asleep. He, too, stretched himself out upon the soft mats, and closed his eyes.

They awoke at the shuffling of feet, and the noise of dishes being brought in. Both enjoyed their supper. It was dark and the rain doors had been closed; but they opened them to enjoy the soft sea breeze. Neither of them spoke, when a whisper came from under the balcony: "Sir, sir, I have brought him."

Inouye recognized the boy's voice. Quietly measuring the height, he took one of the comforters serving as bed, and fastening one end to the railing swung himself over, holding the other end in his hand. A man was standing near the boy, and Inouye asked who he was. The boy told him that he was a sendo. He had found a ship that would leave for Tokyo at dawn, and told her master that two gentlemen at his inn wished to take passage. This sailor had been ordered to show them the way, and to carry their baggage.

Kano and Inouye were highly pleased. They left enough money to pay their bill handsomely, and, after Kano had joined his friend, rewarded the boy. Preceded by the sendo, they made their way to Hyogo and reached the junk in safety. They secured sleeping accommodations, and when they awoke the following morning, and went on deck, they saw that they had left Hyogo far behind.

VIII
YOKOHAMA IN 1859

THE junk had a fair voyage. The passengers who had not been on the ocean before, had suffered from seasickness, but, since the junk generally followed the coast, and often passed through smooth water, they had quickly recovered. The voyage up Yedo Bay had been very pleasant. But they met the tide when they were off Kanagawa, and as there was but little wind, the master had anchored.

If they had known it, they would have looked behind them with some interest, for there was the spot where Commodore Perry had anchored, and with his fire ships, had battered down the door of Japan's isolation. That was five years ago. These five years had brought serious trouble upon their country, and there promised to be graver disturbances; for, as there was restlessness in their clan, so there was restlessness everywhere.

As Kano stood thinking thus, he heard Inouye ask the master of the junk how long it would be before they reached Yedo. The answer was that they must wait six hours before the tide turned, and that then it would take many hours unless the breeze freshened. "But," he continued, "if your honor is in a hurry, I can call a sampan (row boat) and you may be set ashore at Kanagawa. Then you can follow the Tokaido, and reach Yedo to-night."

Kano turned toward the master, and said briefly: "Do so!" A little while after a sampan passed within hailing distance, and soon the two rônin were speeding toward the shore.

Kano and his friend made their way to a quiet yadoya at Noge hill, where they could be sure not to be disturbed by the trains of daimiyo passing to and from the capital, and would be free from impertinent questions. After they had secured accommodations and refreshed themselves with a bath, they took their dinner. Neither spoke of the subject uppermost in his mind, their future plan of action. They were now in the Tokugawa country, and every man might be a spy. Besides, there was no privacy in a house where the walls consisted of sho ji, and even a whisper could be plainly heard in the next room. Therefore, when they had finished their dinner, Kano proposed a stroll. They set forth, and walked in the direction of Yedo. They were sure to be unobserved, since the Tokaido was crowded with travelers of all classes, and samurai were not likely to be questioned after they had passed the barrier.

When they had reached a part of the road where they could talk without danger of being overheard, Kano said:

"We have arrived at the first stage of our journey. Have you thought of any plan to attain our end?"

"I have been thinking, of course," replied Inouye, "but I have no doubt that you have conceived an excellent scheme."

"No, I have not. Every plan I thought of, when I came to work it out, offered some very serious obstacle. I feel as if I am running my head against a stone wall. We may go into Yokohama, and if we are asked who we are, we may answer that we are rônin. But if they ask what we are doing, and we reply that we are curious to see the barbarians, they will say: Very well, you have seen them now, so you had better go about your business. From that time we shall be beset with spies, or we must leave. This is a difficulty which I had not foreseen."

"Your idea is to study the barbarians, is it not?" said Inouye thoughtfully.

"Yes. Our clan must not act blindly. We must know what is the purpose of those men in coming here; but that is not all. We must also know their strength and their weakness."

"There is but one way in which that may be done," muttered Inouye, as if speaking to himself.

"Then that way must be chosen," said Kano. "What is it? You do not hesitate on account of the danger, I hope?"

"No; but I do hesitate on account of the humiliation. Look here, Mr. Kano, I will give you my views frankly. If I were alone, that is, if I had been commissioned by you, I would have left my swords behind, and offered my services to these barbarians in any capacity. I would have entered into such employment as promised the best opportunity to watch them when they were among themselves and off their guard."

"But how would you understand their speech. You do not suppose that they converse in our language, do you?"

"No," replied Inouye, smiling, "but our Japanese interpreters at Nagasaki tell me that it does not take long to learn that tongue, and I do not suppose that there is much difference in the languages spoken by these barbarians."

"Well," said Kano, "I admire your scheme and like it. But such a step requires consideration. Let us return to our yadoya and think it over. To-morrow morning we can decide upon our future action."

When they arrived in their room, the two friends sat down before the hibachi, smoking and sipping their tea. After some time Kano stretched himself on the mats, and was soon sound asleep. Inouye noiselessly opened a sho ji and slipped through, closing it in the same manner. He then went down to the lower floor, and entered the front part of the house which serves as office, kitchen, and as refreshment hall for transient wayfarers of the poorer class.

Here he found the landlord, squatting behind his tiny desk. As Inouye approached, the landlord bowed low, since, although the guest was now dressed in kimono only, and had left his swords up-stairs, he remembered having seen him enter as a samurai. Inouye sat down within easy reach of the landlord, and asked: "How far is it from here to Yokohama?"

"That depends, your honor, upon the way you may choose. Across the new causeway it is about two miles, but it is further by sampan."

"Are there any guards?"

"There were, your honor, but the barbarians made so much fuss about them, that they were withdrawn."

"Then anybody may go in there without any impertinent questions being asked?"

"Oh yes, your honor. The barbarians do not seem to care as to who comes."

"Have you been there?"

"Yes, I have been there twice. When the first barbarians landed I thought that I would go and see how they looked. I was disgusted! Not one of them possessed any manners. They shouted at the top of their voices, pushed and crowded each other, and acted as if they were possessed of demons. It was horrible."

"Then why did you go again?"

"My little son was very sick, and some traveler told me that these barbarians possessed powerful charms. Every physician said that the boy must die, and I thought that I would try to obtain a charm that would save the child's life. So I went to the gate at the causeway and asked where I could purchase those charms. He told me that he did not know, but when he knew what I wanted them for, he advised me to go to an American physician who lives in Kanagawa near the causeway. I did so, and found him at home. He was a tall, powerful man, but very kind. There was a Japanese in his house who could understand me, and when the physician knew what was wanted, he and the Japanese gentleman went with me. When we came home, he asked some questions, examined the child tenderly, and gave it some medicine. He and his friend remained three hours, and only when the child was sleeping peacefully, did he leave. The next day he came again, and the next, and the next, and now the child is as well as ever. And he would not accept any money. All barbarians are not bad men, that is sure, but most of them are very rude."

"Do you know how they live in their homes?"

"No. I have heard some young good-for-nothings of this place who had served them as kodz'kai[49] (attendant, servant) speak about them, but you can not believe what they say. Decent men will not enter their service. Only a few days ago the good physician asked me to get him an honest man, but, although I have tried hard and the wages are high, nobody cares to take the risk."

"Is there any chance to secure work from them in Yokohama?"

"Oh! there is plenty of work, and the pay is good. But our people do not like it much. They have to work too hard. They are not allowed to rest a minute, and when one of them should smoke a pipe for a moment, and he is seen, he receives his pay up to that time, and is sent about his business. If they treat our people in that manner, it will not be long before they will have to do the work themselves."

Inouye agreed with the landlord, and, while that worthy was giving change to a servant girl, he slipped up-stairs. He found Kano still asleep, and sat down before his hibachi thinking deeply. There was absolute silence in the room, save when he knocked the ashes out of his pipe.

It was quite dark when Kano awoke. "What, is it so late!" he said as he looked out on the balcony, and saw the lights of the ships in Yokohama harbor. "I thought I would sleep for an hour or so, and here I have taken a whole afternoon!"

"I am glad of it," replied Inouye. "After supper we must stroll to the beach, for I have much to tell you. I do not think that there will be so very much difficulty in carrying out our plans. But it is best not to speak of them here."

Kano nodded, and clapped his hands as a signal to serve up supper. They spoke about the food, and joked with the servants. After having satisfied their appetites, they strolled to the beach.

It was a calm, bright night; the only noises disturbing the almost oppressive silence, came from the ships in harbor, or from the shrill whistle of the blind shampooer, as he offered his services in the way peculiar to that trade. Kano led the way until they came to a little hillock where they could notice the approach of strangers. He sat down, and courteously motioned Inouye to take a seat by his side. Inouye did so, and at Kano's request related his conversation with their landlord.

He then suggested that Kano should apply for the position of house servant of the barbarian physician, while he, Inouye, would try to secure work at Yokohama. But Kano would not hear of this. "No!" he said. "This physician seems to be a good man; you must go there, and I shall mingle with those rude people at Yokohama. But on ichi-roku nichi[50] we must meet here at eight o'clock, and communicate each other's experiences. But what shall we do with our swords? They would betray us at once?"

"That, certainly, is a difficulty, but not a serious one. Let us think it over, we are sure to find some way out of it."

The two samurai then returned to their inn and retired.

IX
NEW EXPERIENCE

AFTER eating their breakfast at an early hour on the following morning, Inouye went down stairs in search of the landlord. He found him sitting at his desk, as if he had not left it since their last conversation. He called for the bill, and gave such a generous tip that the landlord was highly pleased, and showed it by his repeated and humble bows. Inouye made a suitable reply, and then said:

"Landlord, I have spoken with my elder brother about what you told me yesterday. The Go rojiu is anxious that some of our young men should learn the barbarian language, and we came here to look for the best ways and means, for it was decided in our family that I should try. It seems to me that the easiest way would be to live with them, and after what you have told me about the physician, I think I would like to serve him, and my brother agrees with me. Now, it does not matter who we are, but I am no good-for-nothing, and shall do my duty. For the present my name is Tomori, and I ask you if you will direct me to this physician?"

"I shall do better than that," replied the landlord. He clapped his hands, and when a servant appeared, he told him to bring OKichi[51] San. Soon after the Honorable Master Kichi appeared. "Honorable Master Kichi," said his father to the eight year old urchin, "take this gentleman to the house of the American physician." Kichi bowed, and leading the way, brought Inouye to a private house, off the Tokaido and near the causeway leading to Yokohama. There was a small but well kept garden in front. It was a house which had evidently been built for a well-to-do samurai, but Inouye noticed that the sho ji, instead of being of paper, were of a transparent substance, probably glass.

Kichi pulled the rope of a gong, the sound of which brought a pleasant looking Japanese gentleman to the door.

Inouye bowed, and his salute was returned in the same ceremonious manner. He then asked if he could see the barbarian physician. "I am sorry," said the other, "but he is out. He will be back very soon, I think; be pleased to enter." He showed Inouye the way to a back room, with tatami[52] on the floor, and, after repeating the salutations, said:

"I hope that it is not on account of illness that you wish to see the physician?"

"No," replied Inouye. "I shall tell you frankly what brings me here, for I hope to secure your valuable assistance. I have always had a love for books and knowledge, and am very anxious to study foreign languages. I consulted my elder brother, and we came to Kanagawa together. At the inn we heard how kindly this physician had treated our host, and also that he is in need of a servant. My brother and I thought that if my services were acceptable, I should offer them such as they are."

"You are not a Tokugawa man, I fancy."

"Why should I not be?"

"Because your speech savors from the south," was the answer. "I did not ask you that question from motives of curiosity, but because most of the men who enter into the service of foreigners, are such as are bound to find their way to jail. Every foreigner prefers any servant to one from this neighborhood. What name do you wish to go by? I hear the physician's footstep, and will speak to him at once."

He left the room, but returned quickly, preceded by a bearded man in the full vigor of life. Inouye prostrated himself before the stranger, who said in Japanese which sounded quaint although quite intelligible:

"Mr. Tanaka tells me that you wish to enter my service, and I am willing to try you. You are expected to be here from seven in the morning until nine in the evening, and will receive a salary of five riyo.[53] You shall have a room, which Mr. Tanaka will show you, and you can share the meals with the other servants. If you need anything, ask Mr. Tanaka; or if you want to speak to me, come to my room. I shall expect you to-morrow morning; you can now go and bring here what you may have as baggage."

Inouye prostrated himself again. Tanaka then showed him his room, which was in one of the outhouses, but far more pleasant than his own quarters in Choshiu. Everything was clean. He was then taken to the room where the servants took their meals, and to the bathroom reserved for them. At last Tanaka told him that he could take possession at any time during that day, so as to feel more at home when his duties should commence.

When he had left the physician's house, Inouye hastened back to the inn. He was dazed and did not know what to think. He would tell his new experience to Kano and consult with him. He entered the yadoya, and, answering the smiling landlord's humble welcome with a slight bow, he hurried up-stairs. Kano was evidently expecting him, but showed not the least sign of curiosity. Both saluted as became samurai, and upon Kano's invitation, Inouye sat down and lit his pipe, waiting for Kano to speak first.

"Have you succeeded?"

"I have."

"When will you enter?"

"I have agreed to begin to-morrow morning, but I can occupy my room to-day, and bring in my baggage."

"Then you had better make some purchases. Here are a hundred riyo. Nay, do not hesitate," for Inouye was surprised at such a large sum being offered to him, "for your work is of great value to the clan, and you may need it; something may occur, or you may be suspected, and Choshiu can not afford to lose so worthy a samurai as my young friend Inouye has proved to be." Inouye bowed low, to hide his confusion. It was so rare that a samurai of Kano's rank bestowed praise that Inouye was deeply moved. Kano pretended not to notice the emotion, and continued: "While you are making your purchases after dinner, I shall go to Yokohama and see what success I may achieve. But what shall we do with our swords?"

"I could take them with me to the physician's house."

"Very well. You will wait here for me until I return?"

Inouye bowed assent. Dinner was ordered and brought up; after it was eaten, the two left the house, barefooted and in simple cotton kimono. They went together as far as the Tokaido, where Inouye pointed out the physician's residence. Kano noticed it closely. They then parted, Inouye turning to the left to visit the stores, while Kano descended to the causeway, and followed it toward Yokohama.

It was six o'clock before he returned. Inouye had noticed that Kano had avoided asking for particulars. He, as younger in years, and less high in rank, would have committed a severe breach of good breeding amounting to a crime, if he had asked a question except in explanation. The same ceremonious salutations took place, and supper was ordered. After it was over, Kano said:

"We are now about to part. I am to begin to work to-morrow as a ninzoku.[54] I have been engaged by a fellow, a Japanese, who will have a taste of the lash before I am entirely through with him." The false smile and suppressed emotion with which this was hissed out between his lips, proved how pitilessly in earnest he was. "But we shall reserve our observations for a month from now. We meet every fifth day, as we agreed yesterday. Here are my swords," saluting reverently as he handed them to his companion, who received them with marks of even greater reverence.

Inouye concealed the swords, with his own, among his clothes. He then took the bundle to the door. Here he turned round, and prostrating himself, bent his head three times upon his outstretched hands. Then, rising, he bowed once more, drawing in his breath. Kano replied in the same manner. Not another word was said, and Inouye carried his bundle to the scene of a new life.

Kano remained alone, deeply buried in thought. Not the slightest token of emotion was visible, yet the man was terribly wroth. His long-practised self control enabled him to conceal the passion he felt by that stolid look of contemplation which completely veils the thoughts. He sat motionless, regardless of the time, mechanically answering the servant who arranged the comforters for his couch. The streets were silent, the yadoya had closed up for the night, and still Kano was sitting there motionless as a statue. Midnight was past, when he felt for his tobacco pouch. Stirring up the few sparks in the hibachi with the chopstick-like brass tongs, he took a few whiffs at his pipe, and then, confident that he had schooled himself for the coming ordeal, he lay down upon his couch.

X
FRIENDSHIP OR HATRED?

SIX weeks had passed. It was in the evening after supper, when three samurai were sitting in the room overlooking the garden of Choshiu's yashiki in Yedo. Guards were stationed within easy distance, so as to encircle the principal building, one room of which was occupied by Kano, in virtue of his influence within the clan. It was known that the Go rojiu had scattered more spies about the yashiki of the great southern clans. Kano, who, had arrived only that morning, had immediately ordered the captain of the guard, to produce a list of every person living within the yashiki or its grounds. Together they had scanned every name, and those who were not personally known to the Councillor or the Captain, were served with a notice to depart, and had been escorted to the gate. Kano had also given orders that a report should be prepared at once, explaining who was responsible for their presence. Until this had been sifted to the bottom, a number of young samurai of known loyalty had been selected to guard the palace, in turn, and they had received orders to cut down any one found prowling in the grounds. A search was made under the palace, and it was only when satisfied that floor nor ceiling had been tampered with, that Kano felt he could speak without fear of being reported.

After he was satisfied of his privacy, he had sent word to the guard at the gate that, when Mr. Inouye should arrive, he was to proceed immediately to the palace. The answer was that Inouye was in the yashiki, and in the apartments of Mr. Ito. Kano had then sent a request to the two friends to visit him in his room. They had returned with the messenger, and had taken supper together. The servants had brought tea and tobacco, and had been dismissed.

"Gentlemen," said Kano, "we shall now proceed to business. Mr. Ito, your friend has probably informed you of what has brought him to Yedo?"

"Beyond mentioning incidentally that his visit was connected with business of the clan, he has not done so, your honor."

"That is entirely like *my friend* Inouye. It was like a true samurai, although, in this case, so much caution was superfluous. I am, however, pleased, because I shall have the satisfaction of enlarging upon the merits of our friend."

Inouye bowed to the ground, and protested that he had only acted as every samurai of Choshiu would have done. Kano then proceeded to unfold the events leading to their mission, and their adventures, until the time when they entered upon their novel experiences, while Ito, although deeply interested and astonished, preserved the same placid countenance. Kano continued:—

"We met, as agreed upon, every fifth day. It was, I confess, a relief to me to see a face I could trust, but I would not permit our friend to tell me his experience. It was because I desired facts, and not mere impressions. The investigation regarded the welfare of the clan, hence, of course, no sacrifice could be too great. Above all, the council desired impartial accounts; justice, full justice, must be done to the barbarians and to the Tokugawa, and that the judgment might be unbiassed, time nor expense should be taken into account. I am, even now, sorry that an accident drew the attention of the Tokugawa spies upon me, and compelled me to leave suddenly. It was not difficult to baffle those dogs, and I am quite sure that they lost all traces of me. They are probably burying my body now. It was owing to my supposed death that I could warn our friend here, who will now, I am sure, entertain us with his experience."

Inouye bowed and said: "If I had been permitted to give your honor my impressions, when I was first engaged by that *good* man, the American physician, they would not vary materially from what I can now state as my knowledge. From first to last, he and his family treated me with the greatest kindness. I was known to him as Tomori, the kodz'kai; yet when he *requested* me to do something, it was always with a 'please!' and he invariably thanked me. He observed that I was anxious to acquire his language, perhaps Mr. Tanaka, his interpreter, had told him so. The first day, when the work was done, he sent for me, and, taking a book from his shelves, began to teach me. Thanks to his patience, I can now fairly read and speak his language.

"The work was light; to be sure, it was not the work of a samurai, but I was not made to feel that I was a menial. At first I was shocked when I saw that his wife was really the master in the house, and that he paid her marked deference whenever they met. They ate together and walked out together. But I found out very quickly that, while she directed the affairs of the household, and looked after the children, she did not interfere with his work, except to help him. She looked after all of us, to see that we were made comfortable, and often, when my morning's work was finished, she would say: 'Tomori San, bring your books; perhaps I may be able to help you.' Truly, she is a good woman, as her husband is a good man.

"Everybody in the house was required to come in the dining-room, in the morning before breakfast, and in the evening after supper. When Tanaka came for me the first morning, and I asked him what this meant, he only smiled, and told me to ask again, in about two weeks. I thought it was part of my duty, and, of course, I went. I watched Tanaka, and did as he did. We sat down, and the physician read to us in his own language; what it was, I could not understand. Then they all fell on their knees, while he spoke aloud; at last, he and his family sang, and then we were dismissed. I saw that Tanaka was unwilling to explain, and did not press him. In about two weeks I began to understand some of the words, and then it dawned upon me with horror, that this physician belonged to the jashui mono,[55] the corrupt sect. Then I remembered the edict of Iyeyasu[56]:—'The Christians have come to Japan to disseminate an evil law, to overthrow right doctrine, so that they may change the government of the country and obtain possession of the land. If they are not prohibited, the safety of the state will surely be imperiled; and if those charged with the government of the nation do not extirpate the evil, they will expose themselves to Heaven's rebuke.' I was horror-struck, and felt that, indeed, I was running in danger for the sake of the clan. But that same thought calmed me. What was the danger compared to the clan. And as I grew calmer, I remembered that I did not see any crosses, and that the priests of Iyeyasu's time were not permitted to marry. Still, as my duty permitted me to go into any room, at any time of the day or evening, I watched the physician, his wife and children so closely that they could do nothing without it being known to me. I had my pains for my trouble. I discovered nothing, because there was nothing concealed. I kept watching, I never relaxed until the time I left, because it was my duty to the clan. I have since discovered that the physician and his wife are Christians, but surely there has been either a terrible mistake made, or there are two sorts of Christians. At any rate, they do not belong to any corrupt sect.

"I will now sum up my experience. I have learned their language to a considerable extent. I have learned that there are many foreign nations, differing in language, habits, customs, as much as we differ from those of China and Korea. I have also received from the physician a book which gives the size of each country, the population, the army, navy, and a great many other interesting facts; but I would doubt its accuracy, only the physician tells me that it is very nearly correct. What made me doubt is that, in referring to Dai Nippon, which they called Japan, it is stated that we have two emperors, one spiritual and one temporal, whom they name Tai Kun.[57] When I showed this to the physician, he smiled, and said that it was our fault that foreigners knew so little of our country, because we had never permitted them to come and enjoy its beauty."

Inouye then produced one of the large geographies used in our schools. He showed them the map of the world, and the size of Japan compared with that of other nations. The map of the United States was closely examined, as well as that of the ocean which separates it from Japan. All this was new to Kano and Ito, and both were absorbed in the subject. Inouye explained as much as his limited knowledge of English would permit; although his progress in that language, considering the time he had been able to devote to its study, was simply marvelous. At last Kano requested Inouye to put the book up until some other opportunity. The geography was then carefully wrapped up in cotton, and again in embroidered silk, showing the great value attached to it. Both Kano and Ito asked minutely about the daily life of the physician, whom they did no longer mention as "barbarian," but Oisha-san,[58] Honorable Mr. Physician, a token of the favorable impression made upon them by Inouye's simple account. All these questions were answered promptly, and it was past midnight when Kano broke up the meeting with the words:—

"Gentlemen, this has been a very pleasant evening to me, none the less because I am surprised. My experience is very different from that of Mr. Inouye. I intended to give it to you this evening, but he has beguiled us with his interesting account. The clan will appreciate what he has done: the knowledge he has acquired will be of great usefulness, and his loyalty to the clan deserves recognition."

Kano called a guard to conduct the two friends to their quarters, and all retired to rest.

XI
CHOSHIU'S YASHIKI

THE next morning had been a busy one for Kano. All the officers of the clan, entitled to the privilege, had called to pay their respects. It was eleven o'clock when the Commandant requested an audience. He was admitted, and reported that the evening before one of the younger samurai, returning home from a visit to a Tosa friend, had been grossly insulted by two men; that he had drawn his sword and had killed one and seriously wounded the other. The affair had taken place not far from the yashiki, and the captain of the guard had despatched some men to the scene. The wounded man was carried in and had since died. He bore the Tokugawa crest, and a letter addressed to the Go rojiu was found upon him. The Commandant delivered the letter, and asked what was to be done.

Kano had listened with little interest, only ejaculating sometimes a polite nara hudo![59] to show that he was listening. When he read the inscription,—the name of the sender is always upon the address of a letter,—there was no longer lack of interest. It was from Sawa! Was it a trap or was it fate? His questions showed the importance of the case.

Had the samurai been placed under arrest?

Certainly.

Who is he? 'Hm! a man above reproach.

What are his habits? Regular? Very well, but let him be closely investigated. Enjoin the strictest silence upon the guard. Let the body be placed in a coffin, ready for funeral. Was the man's comrade dead? That was ascertained? Very well. The matter would be duly considered, and instructions would follow in due time.

Kano was toying with the letter. What should he do? This was a business that must be decided by the Council of the Clan. But who constituted the council? Kano smiled, for he was alone. Hattori and himself. Hattori had his own opinions—until he was made acquainted with those of Kano. That was all true, but this was a matter of life and death, and Kano hesitated. Suddenly a thought struck him. "Yes," he thought, "that young man has brains, and thinks for himself; he is the man I need." He clapped his hands, and when the attendant appeared, desired him to invite Mr. Inouye to call at once, and that his friend Mr. Ito should favor him with a visit after dinner.

He had not long to wait before Inouye appeared. Kano at once invited him to enter, and at once told him of the fight and the difficulty it involved.

Inouye's face was expressionless, but when Kano asked him what he would do in this case, he inquired:

"Has your honor examined the samurai?"

Kano replied by requesting him to act as secretary, and together they repaired to the Commandant's quarters. Writing materials were brought, and the prisoner entered.

He was a manly youth, twenty or twenty-two years old. He prostrated himself before the councillor, and, upon being told to give an account of the affair, he told simply that he had applied for and received a pass from the Commandant to visit a friend in the Tosa yashiki. That he had returned home by way of the inner castle wall, and, after crossing the bridge, two samurai had purposely run against him, and called him a lout. He had demanded an apology, whereupon one of them had ordered him upon his knees. At that insult he had drawn his sword, and had duly punished the insolent braggards. He had then returned home, and reported the affair to the Commandant.

Kano had the prisoner removed, but when the Commandant reported that he was of exemplary antecedents and conduct, he was brought in again, and, after exhorting him to keep silence, he was commended for his courage and discharged. The Councillor gave orders to have the body cremated, and returned with Inouye to the Palace.

They had dinner together, and after the room had been cleared, and the servants withdrawn, Kano deliberately opened the letter, and read it. He then handed it over to Inouye, who also read it carefully, returning it to Kano, who said:

"It seems that we must return to Nagato. Sawa's conscience begins to prick him unless the council has stopped his supply of money, or he has been reproved by the Go rojiu. He says in his letter that it is said that I am ill, but that he does not quite believe it. Well, as soon as I get back, I shall invite him to call, and scold him roundly for neglecting me so long. That, and a few hundred riyo, will appease his tender conscience. I wish I could sweep the whole Tokugawa breed from the soil of Dai Nippon! Ah! here is your friend Ito!"

As soon as the expected guest was seated Kano said:

"It is now my turn, gentlemen, to go over my experiences with the foreign devils. Mr. Inouye will remember how I went to Yokohama in search of work. When I arrived, I entered a tea house, and after taking a cup or two, inquired where I might get work. I was directed to the hatoba,[60] where I found a number of ninzoku, moving cases and bales. I asked of one of them who was their employer. He rudely pointed to a man of about my own height, who was scribbling in a book. I went to this person, and offered my services. The rude dog said curtly:—'Wait!' I tell you, gentlemen, it was well that I had left my swords behind, for I came very near forgetting myself; as it was, my palms itched. The people close by seemed accustomed to this sort of treatment, for no one paid attention, except one who looked at me curiously for a moment. After about five minutes, the fellow came up to me, looked me over as you would look over a horse you wished to buy, and then said curtly: 'Come to-morrow at seven. If you are late, you need not come at all,' I said nothing, but promised to teach that fellow manners, before we parted finally. Nevertheless, I was on hand in time the next morning and enjoyed some very wholesome muscular exercise. It was then that I had occasion to notice the first foreign devil. He was a tall and well-built man with reddish hair and beard, and walked as if the earth belonged to him. A small coolie was in his way, and he lifted his foot, and kicked, actually kicked, that poor fellow out of his way. I jumped up as if I had been struck myself, when the same man who had looked so oddly at me the day before, seized me by the girdle, and without looking up, whispered:—'You are forgetting your purpose!' He was right, and brought me to my senses. Well, gentlemen, that day I saw Japanese wantonly struck and knocked down, without any provocation whatever, by several of those foreign devils. At noon most of the coolies ate their lunch where they worked, but the man who had spoken to me came up and said: 'There is a small yadoya close by, shall I show you the way?' I thanked him, and followed. I secured a room and was back in time to train my muscles into whipcord.

"When evening came, I went back to the yadoya, and after taking my bath, had supper. I must say that I enjoyed both more than I ever had before. I was about to lie down, when I remembered that I had not thanked my unknown friend, who decidedly was not what he seemed. I was going down to ask the landlord if he knew him, when I saw him standing in the door. He motioned to follow him; so, securing a lantern from the landlord, I did so. He led the way past many houses built of stone, to a creek. There was a rude bridge, leading to a path ascending to the hills. At the crest he stopped and waited. We were at a point where nobody could approach us unobserved, and he bowed as only gentlemen do. Of course, I returned the salute in the same manner. He then said:—

"'Disguise between you and me is useless. Down below there, I am Eto,[61] a ninzoku; here I am Teraji,[62] a Satsuma samurai, at your service.'

"I have not yet decided what I am down below," I replied, "but at this moment I am Kano of Choshiu, very glad to acknowledge the service rendered to me by the Honorable Teraji of Satsuma."

"'Oh! that is nothing. The situation *is* sometimes a little awkward. I understood your feeling, and was on the lookout. These foreign devils *are* brutal, but it is their nature, I suppose, and they can not help it. But I grieve to notice that this sort of conduct renders our people, who come in contact with them, brutish. They lose all respect for authority and the Tokugawa, or whoever succeeds them in power, is going to have trouble with this class of people.'

"You do not mean to say that the ninzoku are deficient in respect to our authorities?"

"'If they are not yet, they are rapidly growing so. You will notice it yourself. At the same time, you will observe that there is a very great difference among the foreigners. While none of them possess the breeding of a gentleman, there are some naturally wicked, while others have a kindlier disposition. I do not believe that there are many who like to inflict pain. It is easy to perceive that none of them have learned self-restraint, but that they are all under the influence of the passion of the moment. The brute who kicked that poor ninzoku for instance. He was in a hurry, and it was less trouble for him to reach his destination by making room for himself in this manner, than to wait until the coolie could make room for him.'

"What astonished me is that the ninzoku took the attack without resenting it."

"'Well, there are two reasons. Some did resent it at first, but these foreigners are trained to use their fists, and, man for man, our people have no chance. But wait until the coolies grow acquainted. At present they are from the poorest and most thriftless classes of all parts of Japan. Soon, however, they will all be residents of Yokohama, and then they will form into a union. When that time comes I will venture to say that there will be few foreigners who will dare use either fists or feet. But it is getting late. To-morrow we do not work. Every seventh day, the foreigners have a holiday, and we shall be able to take a long walk.'

"We returned to the inn, and parted at the door with a boorish bow. That was the extent of my experience on the first day. It was enough to supply me with food for thought."

XII
SONNO-JOI

KANO rose slowly and left the room. When he returned after a brief absence, he was in kamishimo,[63] a white or hemp-colored dress used only upon the most solemn occasions. He sat down between the two friends, who, astonished as they felt, maintained the same impressive countenance. After thinking for a few minutes, which to Ito and Inouye seemed an age, he resumed:—

"HE WAS IN KAMISHIMO."

"Gentlemen, Mr. Teraji and myself have given the barbarians a fair trial, and we have come to the conclusion that they are not wanted in this fair land of ours. We do not believe that they have any other object in view except trade, but whether they have or not, it is immaterial: they must be expelled. It is the duty of the Shogun to do this, and, were Iyeyasu or Iyemitsu living, I have no doubt the Tokugawa clan would be quite able to accomplish the work in such a manner that the barbarians would think twice before they returned to these shores. Unfortunately, the long peace we have had, has exercised a bad influence upon the Shogun and the clan. Gentlemen, I must trust you entirely. There can be no doubt of the loyalty of Kano to the house of Mori, and yet I dare not repeat, even to my old friend Hattori, what I am about to say to you now. You notice my dress? I put it on because, unless you agree with me, I shall commit seppuku.[64] But pray, give me your close attention.

"It is said, at Nagato, that Kano governs the Choshiu clan, and, in the main it is true, although the other councillors are always consulted. But our Lord Mori is not. He does not know any more about the affairs of the clan, than the ordinary samurai. He is a brave, kind gentleman, who would lead his clan into battle, or commit seppuku, as well as the bravest among us. But he has been trained to have others think for him, and provide for all his wants. That is all very well, so long as peace reigns, and in a small territory like Choshiu. But the same rule prevails in every clan, and not only there, but in the Yedo government. The last Shogun were children, and died young. Iyesáda,[65] the present Shogun, is only a boy. The government is, therefore, conducted by the Go rojiu, and the regent. Ii Naosuke occupies the same position which I hold in our clan.

"I do not know him, but from what I hear, he has brains and courage. He is entitled to those qualities, for his ancestor was one of Iyeyasu's most trusted captains. Yet he has granted all that the barbarians demanded. It has puzzled me, and is puzzling me still, why he did so. Teraji told me that these barbarians had defeated the flower of China's army, and were ready to throw their hosts upon these shores. But the 80,000 samurai of the Tokugawa clans should be strong enough to prevent any army from landing.

"I remember, however, what Mr. Ito told me about the Tokugawa samurai, and my own observation has confirmed his opinion. They are worthless, and a disgrace to us. Why, look at that fellow whose body was cremated yesterday but which should have been thrown to the dogs. He was intrusted with a dispatch, yet engaged in a brawl before executing his commission. Such a man is unworthy of being a samurai. Ii Naosuke must have known this, and submitted out of loyalty to the descendant of Iyeyasu. He, too, labors under great difficulties. The Tokugawa family is divided. Mito,[66] notwithstanding his ancestor's will, hopes to see one of his sons succeed as Shogun. If, then, the barbarians must be expelled, it is not the Tokugawa who are able to do it, and therefore that family must be deprived of their power.

"That is the first step. It will take, however, the united efforts of several clans to accomplish it, and the question is: Can a sufficient number of clans be brought to do the work without jealousy. I think not, unless we can secure the person of Tenshi Sama and thereby use his seal."

Both Ito and Inouye, trained in self-control as they were, could not help giving a start. Kano did not seem to notice it, and continued:

"The seal of Tenshi Sama will be obeyed by every clan. The Regent knows that, and has applied to Kyoto to have the treaties confirmed. Happily, there are some among the Kugé,[67] who do not want Tenshi Sama to be mixed up in this matter. They have replied that 'if there must be treaties with the barbarians, the Go rojiu must see to it that they are admitted into the vicinity of Kyoto.' Therefore, the Regent is sorely disappointed. No doubt, he will make further efforts. But some of us must enter into communication with some Kugé, and prevent his success; and, if there is any possibility of securing possession of the Gosho,[68] it must be done.

"We can not confide our plans to other clans. They would think at once that Choshiu wishes to succeed Tokugawa. Perhaps it does. All we do know is that Iyeyasu, who humbled the proudest clan, humbly begged Tenshi Sama to appoint him as Shogun. If he had not possessed the imperial authority, not even he could have prevented constant revolts. But he did possess it, and that is why my ancestor advised his lord not to join the insurgents. It may be, however, that the time has come to wipe out the clan's disgrace, and my ancestor's death. If so, let Tokugawa look to it! That proud clan shall feel what it is when the hand of the despoiler wields a conqueror's magic wand. Now, gentlemen, I have given you my opinion, and if I have spoken treason, I shall expiate my sin at once and in your presence, that no taint may rest upon my son. If, on the contrary, you agree with me, I need all the help that your devotion to the clan can offer. But perhaps you would like to ask any questions?"

Inouye waited for Ito to speak, but when he perceived his friend to be buried in thought, he said:—

"Perhaps your honor may be willing to explain what caused your hurried departure from Yokohama, and why I was ordered to resign at a minute's notice."

"Teraji was to blame for it," replied Kano, "although I share in the blame. A boy committed an error in piling up cases to be loaded in a ship, and was brutally maltreated by the master. Sorely hurt, he was unable to go on with his work, when the Japanese who engaged me, after ridiculing the lad, gave him such a push that the lad fell and broke his leg. It happened just before the time when we were dismissed for the day, and I found Teraji waiting for me. He told me that he wished to speak to me right after supper, and I knew at once that my sword would be required. So I hastened to Kanagawa, and had no difficulty in securing speech with you. After you had given me my swords, I told you to be at our yashiki here the next day, and returned to the yadoya, where I found Teraji, standing motionless in the shadow of a house. He too, had buckled on his swords, and I scarcely recognized the former ninzoku. We saluted as became gentlemen, and he told me that he was waiting for a messenger. It was almost midnight when a boy appeared, and after looking first at me and then at him, beckoned us to follow. In one of the new streets we saw the master of the ship staggering home. Teraji followed him as a cat steals up to a mouse, crouching, ready for the spring. And as he did leap, out flashed his sword. Satsuma has lost neither nerve nor muscle. There was one barbarian less, gentlemen, and as Teraji wiped his sword upon the clothes of the dog, he said: 'Now let us begone.' 'No, not yet,' said I. This time I took the lead to the house of the Japanese brute. I disliked to soil my dagger in the scoundrel's dirty blood, but I desired to avoid an outcry. When we came to his house, I called him and told him he was wanted at the hatoba. He did not hesitate. We took him through the street where the master still lay, and when he bent over to see who it was, I took care that he did not get up again. When we examined him to see if he was dead, Teraji exclaimed at the likeness with me. To make it appear more so, he helped me to exchange kimono, then I gave a few cuts in his face, and we left him. We made our way unobserved into Kanagawa, and from there to Yedo. Teraji went to Satsuma's yashiki and I arrived here, wholly unobserved, I am sure. I had some little difficulty in convincing our worthy commandant of my identity."

"Then your honor thinks that there is no suspicion among the metsuke of your being here?"

"I think not."

"What orders does it please your honor to give us?"

"Then you agree with me that I am right. That is well. Now, gentlemen, this may cost your lives. The clan must not be compromised. Mr. Inouye has written his resignation, you Mr. Ito must do the same. Inouye must go to Kyoto, and enter into communication with the Gosho. I shall join him there, after I have shown myself to the clan, and given the necessary instructions to my friend Hattori. You, Ito, must visit the clans, as a rônin. Do not spare money. Entertain freely. Tell every samurai who is willing to listen of how the barbarians are desecrating the land of the gods. Be prudent, but raise the battle-cry of Sonno-Joï[69]; Revere the Emperor, Expel the Barbarian! That cry must be heard from Hokaido to Kiu-siu. Yours will not be a difficult task. Our young samurai, except those Tokugawa she-monkeys,[70] are anxious enough to test their blades. You will find many of them willing to provoke a war. Direct them to Kyoto. It will need a very strong cry to awaken the court to action, after its centuries of sleep. But do not supply them with money. We do not want any hirelings within our ranks, we need patriots."

Ito bowed, and said thoughtfully: "Your honor is right in saying that mine is an easy task. There will be no difficulty in raising the cry of Sonno-Joï, nor in getting brawny arms to clasp the hilt of the sword. But who shall stifle the cry or sheath the blades, after they have served the purpose? I have heard of little boys, in the mountains of the north, starting a snowball down the hill; and when it did come down, a whole village lay buried."

"That is so," replied Kano. "But our country has never in vain called for men to guide it in time of danger, nor will it now. One or two clans are powerless to preserve it from the barbarians, but all the clans united, are invincible. Here is an order upon the treasurer. Take an ample supply of money, for you will need it. When will you be ready to start?"

"As soon as your honor commands," replied Ito bowing.

"Do so, then, as soon as possible. Mr. Inouye will keep me company as far as Hyogo. I have a passage engaged by a ship leaving to-morrow. In all our actions let us never forget our motto: Sonno-Joï, Revere the Emperor, Expel the Foreigner!"

XIII
PLOTTING

TWO men, dressed in kimono, haori, and hakama were sitting in one of the numerous temples which add to the natural beauty of the old imperial capital of Japan. The noon meal was over, but neither had an eye for the glorious landscape spread out before them. To the right and left a wave of mountains seemed to roll up in ever increasing height, until those in the background pierced the deep-blue sky. The hills about the city were clad in a mantle of green of every shade, from the dark needles of the fir to the light shoots of the bamboo. Crag and cliff bore the crimson torii, the unique indication of the proximity of temple or shrine. Yonder, at their feet, lay the holy of holiest, the Gosho, the residence of Tenshi Sama, the representative of the Yamato Damashii,[71] the fierce Spirit of Old Japan. A fierce spirit! Men trained to consider duty the sole motive, reckless of pain, and inured to the sight of blood, are not sparing of that precious fluid when they are bent upon the execution of a purpose. Yet the recluse yonder, the very incarnation of that spirit, dwelling in the temple-like building surrounded by enchanted gardens, seemed unconscious of his power to stir millions of brave men into action, by a mere use of his seal.

"Then his lordship thinks that it can be done?" asked Inouye, for he was one of the occupants of the room.

The man thus addressed, bowed low, and said:—"My master has sent your honor a haori with his crest. I passed through the gate, and left my name ticket; then pretending that I had forgotten something, went in again, and when I came out I deposited the ticket of Mr. Kida, a distant relative, who was admitted in the service of my master. It is time that we should go. If your honor will put on this haori, and, upon entering the gate, demand Kida's ticket, there will be no difficulty."

Inouye dressed, and the two descended toward the city. The road passed by one of the Gosho gates, and the guide entered, exclaiming his name, whereupon he received a wooden ticket with his name in large characters, and passed through. Inouye followed his example, and received a similar ticket bearing the name of Kida. The two then walked up a broad gravel path toward one of the enclosures.

Notwithstanding all his self control, Inouye experienced great difficulty in not betraying his intense curiosity. He, as every Japanese of his class, thought with intense reverence of Tenshi Sama. His heart would have leaped for joy if he had received orders to die that moment for the man he had never seen. We can not understand that feeling. Loyalty is a meaningless sound compared to it. Yet it was that feeling which metamorphosed a federacy of some three hundred autonomous oligarchies, poverty stricken and at war with one another, into a powerful empire which bids Russia defiance. This marvel, too, was accomplished in less than three decades!

Inouye's curiosity was, therefore, blended with awe. The guide stopped before a house of modest dimensions, but of light and elegant construction, and, bowing, preceded his companion. Stopping on the verandah, he uttered his name in a low but distinct voice. An answer was returned, and he beckoned Inouye to enter. The latter did so, and, prostrating himself, ejaculated rapidly such phrases of self-depreciation as the high rank of a Kugé demanded.

Karassu Maru,[72] the master of the house, was a young man of about Inouye's age, dressed in haori, hakama, and kimono all of fine silk. He scanned Ito's features keenly, and appeared satisfied with the result. He was evidently of a quick, impulsive temper, but used the courtly language, and strictly observed his own dignity.

"I am informed that you have a proposition to place before me on behalf of Mori.[73]"

"I am but the messenger, My Lord, and my authority extends only to requesting an audience of your lordship for the first councillor and friend of my Lord Mori."

"But, you know, there is some danger in coming to and going from the Gosho. Our friends of the Aidzu Clan, whom the Go rojiu has kindly deputed to guard us here, seem to scent danger, for they have drawn the lines tighter and tighter. It would be better if I knew something of what Mori wishes, so that both time and risk could be saved."

"I will tell you, my lord, what I know."

Inouye then gave a comprehensive but concise review of Kido's intentions, reserving, of course, the conclusions of his leader, and the share he intended to assign to the Gosho. Karassu Maru listened attentively, and when Inouye concluded, he said:

"When do you expect the councillor of your clan?"

"He will come, your Lordship, as soon as I let him know that he may have an audience."

"I am willing to hear him, but he will need great powers of persuasion. Of my personal friends, one is an idiot, and the other a fool. No; I can't do a thing, although I would like to try. The affair ought to be begun by one of the Miya,[74] but that is altogether out of the question. Ni-jo?[75] bah! he would not stir. Sanjo? Yes, he might. Aye, I think that he would. Hold on! There is Tomomi. He is the man!"

This was evidently not destined for the ears of Inouye, who was listening but without any expression in his features. Karassu Maru looked up, and said:—

"See that Mori's councillor is here on the tenth day from now. The same retainer who brought you here will call for him, and I shall arrange a meeting. Now about getting out. He clapped his hands, and when the attendant appeared, he said: 'Get the football ready, and invite Honami and Gojo with their retainers to join me in a game. You, sir, come along. When we come to the wall near the gate the guard will be watching us. See to it that you do not kick it over the wall, for I am a good hand at scolding, and you would not care to be called clumsy, would you? If, however, you should send it flying over the wall, run after it, and throw it back. We shall entertain the guard.'"

It was dark when Inouye returned to the temple, but he wrote at once to Kano. The letter was foolish, and made the writer appear to live only for amusement. It described the magnificence of the temples and urged Kano to be present at a festival to take place on the tenth day. There was nothing in it of the slightest interest to any spy.

Kano was at home when the letter was delivered to him. He saw, after a close examination, that it had been opened, but smiled after he had read its contents. He knew the spy. Why had Sawa so earnestly requested him to admit among his retainers a young friend who had some slight trouble in his own clan? Kano had demurred to keep up appearances, but finally he had agreed, and he knew that there was no longer any privacy in his house. It was immaterial to him. He did not know of one member of his clan in whom he could trust. Not that there was any doubt whatever of their loyalty, but one thoughtless word or action would upset all his plans. He was glad that he had two such friends as Ito and Inouye. Sonno-Joï! Why he had heard that cry in his own clan, here at the confines of Hondo. There had been no communication from him, and this was the first that he received from Inouye. Truly, there was a chance for Choshiu when the clan numbered among its members such men. O! if Ekichi might only grow up to such a standard.

He clapped his hands and ordered the child to be called. The boy came, knelt at the threshold, and saluted his father with the reverence due to him, and the gravity of a man. Kano bowed in return, and said:—

"Come here."

The boy came, bowed, and squatted down.

"Are you doing well at school?"

Ekichi bowed.

"Read that to me," he continued, taking up a book. The boy began to read in the sing-song tone necessary to render ideographic writing intelligible to the reader. His father then inquired after his progress in athletic exercises, and finally said: "Come, we shall go into the garden!"

They walked together to an artificial hillock, found in every Japanese garden of any pretensions, and ascended to the top. Here, safe from spies, Kano turned to his son:

"Listen, Ekichi," he said. "You know the new attendant who came here some months ago?" The child bowed. "Very well; I want you to be the shadow of that man. He must not be anywhere, or you must see him; he may not say a word, or you must hear what it is. I am going away for a few weeks, and when I am back, you must read on this hillock every afternoon, until I come up, and then you must tell me what this man has done, whom he has seen and what he has said. Can you do that do you think?"

The little fellow felt overjoyed at this token of his father's confidence, but not a look betrayed that feeling. He accepted the charge with a simple bow, and went with his father back to the house.

Kano dressed, and ordered his chair. When he entered it, he said briefly: "To the castle!" Alighting at the inner entrance, he distinctly ejaculated his name; a servant appeared and bade him enter.

The room was almost the same as his sitting-room in his own house. There was no furniture, but a kakemono,[76] of priceless value in Japanese eyes, hung from the wall so that the light fell upon it. A few bronze pieces, masterworks of art, stood where they appeared to demand admiration. In the middle of the room sat the owner of the estate, an estimable gentleman of middle age, dressed in magnificent silk. Kano saluted dutifully and was bidden to approach. He sat down at the prescribed distance, and waited for his master to address him.

"I am glad you called," said Mori. "I want the garden changed, and my cousin told me that the council had appropriated too much money for the fortifications at Shimonoseki. What fad is this? Those works were constructed under my grandfather, and could not be made better. It is more important by far that the garden be altered. Come here! Do you not see that if I sit here and look out, that hillock yonder interrupts the view? It must be changed."

Kano bowed low and said: "It shall be done, my lord. I am going to Kyoto on business for the clan. Is there anything I can do for you?"

"Why, certainly. If you can pick up any fine antiquities, do so. And you must order new haori for the retainers. They will need them on our next journey to Yedo."

Kano promised to attend to these matters, and took his leave. Closing the sho ji behind him, he went to a distant part of the palace, and called an attendant. "Request Mr. Hattori to come here," he said. Hattori came, and his friend told him that he was called to Kyoto on private business, and would be absent for two or three weeks. He requested him to see that the garden was altered according to the wishes of the Lord of the Manor. Hattori promised to comply. Kano then proceeded to Sawa's yashiki, and told him that he had come to bid him good-bye, as he was going to Kyoto under orders from my lord to buy some new ornaments. He asked for a letter to the commandant of the castle at Kyoto, a request which was willingly granted. When Kano left, a small bag of gold remained on the cushion which he had occupied.

XIV
WITHIN THE PALACE

IN one of the kuge residences, not far from the palace occupied by the Tenshi sama, four men had just exchanged the protracted salutations prescribed by their rank. All knew that this very meeting would be considered as treason if it were known to the authorities at Yedo, and they felt, intuitively, that it would exercise a great influence upon their lives. Yet every face bore but one expression, that of placid contentment.

Sanjo, as the highest in rank, spoke first:—"His Lordship, Karassu Maru has informed us that the chief Councillor of Mori desires to make a communication. It is long since the chief of a clan desired the intercession of a kuge."

Kano bowed:—"It is the fault of the Tokugawa, My Lord. The clans are shut out from Kyoto. We are not permitted to occupy our yashiki here, unless we secure the gracious consent of the men who rule at Yedo. I know none of the old families, Mori, Shimadzu,[77] who would not willingly enroll himself among the lowest servants of the Son of Heaven. If you are robbed of the homage which is your due, surely we suffer more severely by being shut out from the sacred presence."

Sanjo bowed, and looked at Iwakura Tomomi, who said:—"You speak well, Sir Knight, and we do not hold the clans responsible for their compulsory neglect of His Majesty. But we shall be glad to hear what it is that Mori of Nagato desires of us."

"Your Lordships, the Tokugawa has admitted barbarians within the realm of the divine ancestors. They are now upsetting all our time-honored customs at Kanagawa, and demand admittance at Hyogo. Your humble servant has dwelt for six weeks among them. I desired to study them, because I was anxious to know if their unhallowed presence foreboded evil to our country. I am convinced that it does. The five relations[78] upon which our social system rests are disregarded and set at nought by them. They respect nothing we respect. They are rude and insolent, and act as if the country of the gods was theirs by right of conquest. They defy our laws. Who ever heard of a merchant talking back to a samurai? Not only do they do this, but they dare order them about."

"Have you seen that yourself?" asked Sanjo.

"I have, my Lord."

"And what did the Tokugawa Knights do?"

"They did as they were bidden; they obeyed the orders of the insolent dogs."

"Was no complaint brought?"

"Who would bring a complaint, and before whom? The samurai is not accustomed to seek protection. He protects, and in such a quarrel, his good sword is both judge and executioner. But, alas! the Tokugawa samurai is no longer a knight. He has forgotten the existence of the word duty, and has substituted the word pleasure. The country is no longer safe under the guidance of the Tokugawa. It must be taken away from them."

"And given to Mori?" asked Karassu Maru.

"That may be decided later, my lord," said Kano calmly. "At present it is not a question of who shall rule with Tenshi Sama's consent, but if the country shall be safe from the invasion of the barbarians. They may not come in large numbers for some years; but if they upset all our sacred customs, they can ruin Japan without any armed invasion. They are but few in number now, your lordships, and we can expel them. But if we wait for a few years, they will have obtained such a foothold that we may not be able to succeed."

"But what can we do?" asked Iwakura.

"Your lordship, there is but one way. Tenshi Sama may order the Tokugawa to expel the barbarians, the order will not be obeyed, because the clan can not do it, and will not entrust the work to other clans. But Tenshi Sama can give an order to all the clans to do it, and I know of some who will obey His Majesty's orders, regardless of consequences."

"But," said Sanjo, "you know that Tokugawa is Shogun; all orders must be issued to him; such is the law and the custom."

"But if Tokugawa can not, or will not obey?"

Here was a supposition which was very unpalatable, and the three kuge were silent. Orders had been issued from the Palace before, and had been disregarded, but the kuge had been respectfully assured that they had been obeyed. Iwakura knew of one instance, and the angry blood appeared almost through the thick coating of self-control and restraint. At last Karassu Mara said:

"What would you have us do?"

"Send peremptory orders to the Go rojiu, and let the clans know that such orders have been sent."

"Do you know, Sir Knight," he asked, "how we are situated here? Aidzu, one of the Tokugawa clans that will fight, confound it! has a guard at every gate. Not a soul goes in or out, but they know who he is, and I shall be very much astonished and glad for your sake, if you return home without some disagreeable encounter. Why! They discovered after your messenger had left that a stranger had been in the palace grounds, and there was a fine hue and cry. The captain of the guard came to me and dared ask questions; I don't think he will do it again, for I made him understand the difference between a kuge and a dog. We could contrive, perhaps, to send a secret order. But an open order to the clans! Why, that messenger must be nimble-footed who could get as far as one hundred yards from the gate!"

"No!" said Sanjo, "that suggestion is worthless. Mark you, Sir Knight, I do not deny that the Tokugawa hand has rested heavily upon the Gosho, but under whatever circumstances, the Court has maintained its dignity. Nor would any infringement be permitted. Besides, while it is true that his Lordship Iwakura and myself are members of the Inner Council, we are but two, and the majority is composed of old men, wedded to the secluded, contemplative life we lead. If you have no other suggestion to offer, I am afraid that we can not help you."

"But, my Lord," said Kano, "surely, that life of seclusion and contemplation ends as soon as the barbarians land at Hyogo. They are, even now, clamoring to be admitted into Yedo. It is only a question of time, perhaps of very brief time, before they will demand admittance in Kyoto, and from what I have seen of them, they will not show any respect for the Sacred Enclosure."

Karassu Maru grasped the hilt of his sword, while Iwakura and Sanjo were startled.

"Ah! That must be prevented at any cost!" said the former, and Sanjo bowed assent.

After a few moments Iwakura made a movement indicating the termination of the audience, saying: "Sir Knight, we shall report our conference to the Council. We do not pretend to know what the result will be, but I suppose that, if we wish to communicate with you, his lordship Karassu Maru will know how to reach you." Deep bows and sucking of the breath followed, and Kano left escorted by Karassu Maru, who led the way to a secluded part of the grounds.

"Now then, Sir Knight, what do you think of the prospect? Encouraging, is it not? And the two gentlemen whom we have left just now, are the most progressive. Now, let me give you a hint. The Miya and kuge, I say it with all respect, have taken root into the ground. That root must be torn up by main force, before they will move. Pull the ground from under them and you will succeed. If you can not find means to do that, return to your clan and prepare to defend yourself. By the way! Are you acquainted with a gigantic Satsuma knight, who loves the Tokugawa as much as you do?"

"I am not, my Lord," said Kano, surprised.

"Well, he, too, is in hiding in some temple. Hunt him up, and work together. Two can do more than one. Now, how are you going to leave here?"

"I saw a nosimono going to one of the palaces a moment ago, is it going beyond the gate?"

"Yes, that is his lordship Honami, who is so exceedingly bright that he can go wherever and whenever he pleases, but why?"

"Can not your lordship arrange that I shall be one of the bearers?"

"Why, certainly. Come this way and wait in that copse." Karassu Maru returned after half an hour's absence, evidently in great glee. He said that Honami had consented to carry a package to the temple where Inouye had rooms. Karassu Maru then handed to Kano a chair-bearer's coat, and kerchief to tie around his head. It took only a minute to change the clothes, and to make a bundle of haori, hakama, kimono, and swords. A little later Honami's well-known nosimono passed through the gate borne by four stalwart men. When it returned there were only three. One had been lost, and poor Honami's privileges were curtailed, while the other chairbearers were subjected to a severe but useless examination.

XV
UNDERGROUND RUMBLING

THE Choshiu Clan was by no means alone in taking the alarm at the admittance of foreigners. The Japanese, as a nation, possess a dual character, which was typified in their government. Just as the Gosho at Kyoto presented the highest degree of refinement attained by the nation, as well as the amiability, natural kindness, and light-heartedness of the people, so did the Camp at Yedo picture the sterner side of their character inculcated and developed to the utmost in the samurai. But the samurai shared with the people the curiosity which is a national characteristic, and many had visited Yokohama for the sole purpose of examining and taking the measure of these strangers. The early history of that open port, is one of bloodshed. Numerous are the names of foreigners in the graveyard upon the bluff, with the inscription: Murdered. Yet in not one single instance was the perpetrator brought to justice. Not one of these murders was for the purpose of robbery; in every instance the sharp sword had been used to avenge some real or fancied insult.

Except the missionaries who arrived as soon as Japan was opened, there were few, very few foreigners who made any effort to propitiate this people. Most of them had lived for some time in China, where they had met a submissive people. They treated the Japanese in the same manner, with very unexpected results. The resentment turned from the foreigners upon the government which had admitted them, and the Tokugawa dynasty was doomed.

But of the Genrô, the statesmen of revolutionary time, no one had any thought of uniting Japan into an Empire under the direct rule of Tenshi Sama. They knew of no history save that of their own country, and that demonstrated the Son of Heaven as too sacred a person to be troubled with mundane affairs. All desired a strong country under a strong Shogun. There is not the least doubt that Satsuma, Choshiu, and Tosa, to whom Japan chiefly owes its present greatness, worked with that end in view. Nor does it detract from their credit that probably each worked with the ultimate hope to see his own clan take Tokugawa's place. There was not an atom of selfishness in this. The chief impulses constituting our motives in life, the acquisition of wealth and honor or fame, were unintelligible to the Japanese at that time.

Kano returned to the temple, where he had left his chair and bearers, for he was stopping at the Choshiu yashiki, and entered the room where Inouye was waiting for him. Having satisfied himself that there were no listeners, he briefly summed up the result of his interview with the kuge. "There will be no opening of Hyogo," he said. "The Court will move heaven and earth, before it concedes that demand. But Karassu Maru is right. The ground must be pulled from under them, before they will abate one jot of their dignity, such as they understand it. By the way. Go back to Nagato as soon as you can. The attention of the spies will be drawn toward this temple, because one of the bearers of Honami's chair disappeared here. I shall follow you in a few days."

The two devoted samurai reached their own province in safety, and the affairs of the clan continued peaceably, except that a considerable number of young samurai resigned as members of the clan, and disappeared. It was not generally known that their names were not stricken off the rolls, but that the letters of resignation were held in a safe place, in case of emergency. Nobody heard from Ito; at least not directly. Indirectly the cry of Sonno Joï! growing more and more common, showed that he was still gathering recruits in the ranks against the Tokugawa.

Kano smiled grimly when he received from Yedo a copy of a letter sent by the Court to the Daimiyo of Mito. "The Bakufu" (Camp or Yedo Government) it ran "has shown great disrespect of public opinion in concluding treaties without waiting for the opinion of the Court, and in disgracing princes so closely allied by blood to the Shogun. Tenshi Sama's rest is disturbed by the spectacle of such misgovernment when the fierce barbarian is at our very door. Do you, therefore assist the Bakufu with your advice, expel the barbarians, content the mind of the samurai, and restore tranquillity to his Majesty's bosom."

The wedge had entered, but time was required before it could be driven deeper. Kano had gradually prepared his friend Hattori to share his hopes and fears, and effective improvements had been made in the fortifications on the coast of Nagato. Cannon, not of very modern make, but decidedly better than the rusty fire pieces of old, had been purchased at Nagasaki and smuggled in at Shimonoseki; a supply of powder was also procured, and several companies of young samurai practiced daily with the guns. Ekichi had attached himself to Inouye and was rapidly growing into an expert swordsman.

One evening, in the beginning of April, Kano was sitting in his room, talking to his son. The rain doors were up, for it had been blowing hard all day, and it looked like rain. Kano began to think that it was time to retire, when Ekichi told him that there was a knock at the rain doors. Kano took up a lantern, and went on the verandah, when he heard a muffled voice calling him. He opened a door and asked who was there, when he recognized the voice of Ito. He gladly invited him to enter, and reclosing the door, led the way to his room. After the customary salutations, seeing that Ito was cold and wet, he ordered dry garments to be brought, and then inquired when he had arrived. Ito replied that he had come straight to Kano's yashiki, and then asked him if he had heard the news. He received a negative answer and said:—"Before I tell you what it is, I must warn you that you have a spy in the house."

"O! I know that, but he is harmless."

"Yes; he is harmless now; but he must have found out something because the Go rojiu dogs were hot on my trail."

"Ekichi," said Kano, "watch around the rooms; and if you see any one trying to listen, silence him."

The boy bowed and slipped out.

Ito sipped a cup of tea, and, seeing that Kano expected him to speak, said:

"Ii Naosuke is dead."

"Is that so? When did he die?"

"He was assassinated in Yedo on the 23rd of last month."

Kano knocked the ashes out of his pipe, put it up, and looked for further particulars. Ito continued:—

"It was blowing a severe storm in Yedo that day. There was rain and sleet, and sometimes it snowed very heavily. The streets within the moats of the castle are almost always deserted, but this time they were wholly so on account of the weather. It appears that there was some meeting at the castle. At all events the Daimiyo of Kii and Owari with their respective retinues were marching across the bridge into the inner walls, when the retinue of the Lord Regent also approached. The last of the Kii samurai had just left the bridge when the head of Ii's retinue reached it. Several men in rain coats had been loitering; they flung off their coats and as samurai in full armor, attacked the regent's escort. These men were taken unawares, and before they could drop their rain coats a number of them had been killed and Ii was dragged out of his nosimono, and decapitated. Several of the assailants lost their lives, but the leader escaped with the head. It is said that they were Mito rônin."

Kano was silent for some time. At last he said: "This is a death blow for the Tokugawa, for Ii Naosuke was the only man, so far as I know, who could have propped up that falling house. For that reason I am glad. But I am sorry too, for Ii was a patriot. I disagreed with him, but he may have been right when he said, in defense of the treaty which he had made: 'Let us have intercourse with foreign countries, learn their drill and tactics, and let us make the nation united as one family.' I do not think that he could have succeeded, but—"

There was a stifled cry and a blow. A moment later a sho ji opened, and Ekichi came in holding in one hand the bleeding head of the spy, and in the other his drawn sword. The boy said simply: "I have silenced him."

Kano and Ito both looked at the boy. He stood there, waiting patiently until his father should address him. Ito, however, took some paper from his sleeve, and placed it upon the woodwork of the grooves, motioning Ekichi to put the head on it. The boy did so, and Kano told him to come near and tell him what had happened.

"I have watched him several times, as you told me to, when he was trying to listen, and once when he was looking over some of your papers. Every time he made some excuse, but I did not answer him. A few moments ago, I passed into that room, and saw his form crouching before the sho ji. You had ordered me to silence him, and I did so."

Kano said a few words in praise, and bade him go to sleep. Ekichi bowed and withdrew.

Kano went out of the room and in a few moments returned with Fujii. The old man looked grimly at the head as he took it up. The body was removed, and the bloodspots cleaned. It was merely an incident in the life of old Japan.

XVI
THE COURT AROUSED

THE death of Ii Naosuke decided Kano to return to Kyoto with his friends, Ito and Inouye, as he said grimly "to help pull the ground from under the feet of the Court." His acquaintance with Karassu Maru was of material assistance to him. This kugé was of a very impulsive temperament, with none of that self control, characteristic of the samurai. Generous to a fault, he was implacable as a foe. While he frightened some of the more timid kugé by the boldness of his speech, he attracted others. The Court mustered the courage to summon the Shogun to Kyoto, to answer the charge of misgovernment brought against him by several clans. No Shogun had deigned doing homage to Tenshi Sama since 1634. The humble reply from the Go rojiu was followed by another command, in which it appeared plainly that Tenshi Sama's advisers would not entertain a thought of his assuming the government. It said:—

"Since the barbarian vessels commenced to visit this country, the barbarians have conducted themselves in an insolent manner, without any interference on the part of the Yedo officials. The consequence has been that the peace of the empire has been disturbed and the people have been plunged into misery. Tenshi Sama was profoundly distressed at these things, and the Go rojiu on that occasion replied that discord had arisen among the people, and it was therefore impossible to raise an army for the expulsion of the barbarians, but that if His Majesty would graciously give his sister in marriage to the Shogun that then the court and camp would be reconciled, the samurai would exert themselves, and the barbarians would be swept away. Thereupon His Majesty good-naturedly granted the request and permitted the Princess Kazu to go down to Yedo. Contrary to all expectations, however, traitorous officials became more and more intimate with the barbarians and treated the imperial family as if they were nobody; in order to steal a day of tranquillity they forgot the long years of trouble to follow, and were close upon the point of asking the barbarians to take them under their jurisdiction. The nation has become more and more turbulent. Of late, therefore, the rônin of the western provinces have assembled in a body to urge the Tenshi Sama to ride to Hakone, and, after punishing the traitorous officials, to drive out the barbarians. The two clans of Satsuma and Choshiu have pacified these men and are willing to lend their assistance to the court and camp in order to drive out the barbarians. The Shogun must proceed to Kyoto to take counsel with the nobles of the court, and must put forth all his strength, must despatch orders to the clans of the home provinces and the seven circuits, and, speedily performing the exploit of expelling the barbarians, restore tranquillity to the empire. On the one hand, he must appease the sacred wrath of Tenshi Sama's divine ancestors, and, on the other, inaugurate the return of faithful servants to their allegiance, and of peace and prosperity to the people, thus giving to the empire the immovable security of Taisan."[79] (Ta shan—Great Mountain, the Sacred mountain of China.)

The effect of Kano's visit to the Gosho is plainly visible in this document. Iyemochi, the Shogun, paid homage to the Tenshi Sama in April 1863, and the same year released the Daimiyo from their compulsory residence at Yedo. At the same time Kano at last secured the long coveted imperial order to commence the expulsion of the barbarians, and he returned to Nagato in high glee.

In the south-western part of the main island of Japan, known as Hondo, a narrow strait separates it from the island of Kiusiu. This strait is named after the city of Shimonoseki,[80] situated on the northern shore, in Nagato. This shore is composed of bold bluffs, formed of solid rock, covered, however, with abundant verdure owing to ample moisture and the heat of the sun. These bluffs control the strait which forms the western entrance to the Inland Sea, and is used by all vessels plying between Japan and China as offering a safe and quick route. It was here that the Choshiu clan had reconstructed its fortifications, and supplied them with new cannon. The clan had also purchased at great expense two sailing vessels and a steamer and was thus, as the Council thought, well equipped to expel the handful of barbarians.

"THE FRIENDS WERE STANDING IN A GARDEN OF A TEAHOUSE."

In the beginning of July, 1863, the friends were standing in the garden of a teahouse, whose upper story overlooked the entrance to the strait, when an attendant appeared and informed them that a barbarian vessel was approaching. The party went up-stairs and watched the ship, as, unable to stem the current, she came to anchor. "She is going to stay there all night" said Kano grimly. "Well, we don't want any more foreigners nor their vessels, and we will give that one yonder a hint not to come back again." He went out around the batteries and ordered the officers to open fire as soon as it should be light enough.

There was grim expectation among Choshiu's samurai at the prospect of an early battle. They had imbibed the dislike of Kano, and the cry of Sonno Joï had excited them. Still, they retired to rest as usual, but were up with the first dawn. The American bark, the *Pembroke*, was not expecting any hostilities. When the tide turned in the morning, the captain gave orders to hoist the anchor, when he was startled by firing and a moment later a ball went through one of his sails. He had the American flag hoisted, but it produced no effect, except that more batteries opened upon her. The two sailing vessels and the steamer appeared to be preparing to increase her danger, but the sailors worked with a will, and soon had her under weigh. The marksmanship of the Choshiu gunners, however, was very poor, and the *Pembroke* escaped.

It is scarcely credible that Choshiu intended to destroy an unarmed vessel; it is more likely that they meant the firing as a warning to keep away. Kano was satisfied at the effect which he thought had been produced. On the morning of the 16th, about ten days after firing upon the *Pembroke*, he was called by one of his retainers, and informed that a steamer was coming toward the Strait from the Inland Sea. After dressing himself hastily, he went to one of the bluffs where he could observe and at the same time issue orders. He soon perceived that it was a war vessel, and sent Ekichi down to the ships at anchor under the bluff to instruct them to clear for action. He then ordered Ito and Inouye to take charge of two of the batteries, and to open fire as soon as possible. The barbarian ship, however, did not remain in the channel, but made at once for the bluff, where, since the guns could not be sufficiently depressed, she was safe from the batteries. She immediately engaged Choshiu's vessels, and, although the samurai were anxious to fight and to come to close quarters, they could scarcely inflict any damage upon their opponents, because they had not been drilled to this sort of warfare. Kano was furious when he saw his expensive ships destroyed, and he was more angry still when Capt. McDougal of the saucy U. S. Sloop-of-war *Wyoming* by a few parting shots destroyed one of the batteries, and then steamed away, apparently none the worse for her late encounter. It did not improve his temper, when the breeze carried the laughter of some of the barbarian sailors to his ears.

After the *Wyoming* had steamed away, Kano sent for his two friends, and together they discussed the event of that morning.

"It is easy to understand," he said, "why our ships suffered defeat. Our samurai can scarcely be expected to learn to handle strange craft in so short a time. What puzzles me is that we could not sink her with our batteries."

"Why," said Ito, "that was plain enough. She steamed straight under us and for the vessels. If we had been able to loosen the rock, we might have sunk her by letting it fall, but if we had depressed our guns, the shot would have fallen out of them."

"Then they are cowards!" Kano cried, "they knew that we could not hit them there, and so crept under shelter. I don't call that honorable warfare."

"I don't see that," said Inouye smiling. "It is fair in war to take every advantage over an enemy; besides, it was decidedly no coward who would come with one small vessel and attack three, while facing the guns of our batteries. No! We lack the skill. Suppose we put armor on our peasants and arm them with our swords, would they be able to fight as well as we, who are trained from our youth? The biggest and most powerful peasant, in armor, would not be a match for Ekichi. It is the same thing in this case. We have the weapons, but we do not know how to use them."

"We fired well enough when she was in the channel," objected Ito.

"Yes, but you confessed yourself that you could not depress your guns, while that fellow raised his cannon high enough to bring the whole battery about my ears. I don't call it unfair, but it was a very one-sided affair."

XVII
A CONFERENCE

A FEW days after the experience gained in the conflict, Kano decided to go to Kyoto. He announced his decision to the Council, where no opposition was made. Indeed, several members, Hattori among the number, declared that they too would go. They felt that the Clan had thrown down the gauntlet, and that there must be victory or annihilation. There had been a steady emigration of the young samurai, and even Ekichi had besought his father to let him go. It was decided that all should be recalled and ordered to report at Choshiu's yashiki at Kyoto.

When Kano, accompanied by his friends, and escorted by a corps of six hundred well-armed samurai arrived at the Capital, he could scarcely credit his senses. The quiet and almost solemn city had changed apparently into a garrison town. Everywhere samurai were met. The crests of Satsuma, Choshiu, Tosa, Hizen, and Kaga, jostled with those of the Tokugawa, with the result that brawls and street fights were common, and peaceable citizens scarcely dared leave their houses. The shout of Sonno Joï was heard everywhere and at all hours. A revolution was imminent.

It was not long after Kano was installed in his apartments of the yashiki when an attendant announced a visitor, who declined giving his name. Receiving directions to admit him, a samurai in rônin dress, that is without crest and his face concealed by a cloth entered. After saluting, the visitor discarded his disguise, and Kano recognized the features of Karassu Maru.

"Well, Mr. Councillor," said the Kuge after they were seated, "you have indeed heeded my advice of pulling the ground from under the court; you have produced chaos, my friend. What has struck Aidzu, I can not conceive. Our chairs go in and out of the palace gates and, instead of being stopped and turned back, we are politely saluted by the guard. There must be more of this, and I believe Tenshi Sama will order the Phœnix Car, and promenade in the city. But how do you propose to restore order out of this chaos?"

Kano did not confide enough in his visitor to disclose his plans. He replied: "Before building a new house, my lord, it is best to clear away the debris, especially after a conflagration. But, as your lordship knows, I have been at Nagato for some time, and am very anxious to know what has happened. I shall feel much relieved if you will inform me."

"I do not know how it came to pass, but after Iyemochi's visit it was easier for the palace attendants to secure passports, and finally they were no longer demanded. Sanjo, Iwakura, and myself, went in and out as we pleased, and I met a great many rônin, all good fellows. Sometimes we had a little bout, and swords were drawn. Taken altogether, there is a very pleasant change in our condition, and I only hope it will last."

Kano saw that Karassu Maru would not help him much in his scheme. When his visitor departed, he called Inouye:

"Have you still the haori which Karassu Maru lent you?"

"I have, my lord."

"Very well; I have mine. Let us see if they will carry us past the gates of the Gosho."

The two gentlemen went out. Although they met numerous parties of boisterous samurai, they were not molested, since the crest they wore was known as that of a kuge. When they came to the gate, Kano walked boldly in, followed by Inouye.

"Your tablets, please, gentlemen," said one of the guards, bowing.

"How now, fellow," cried Kano haughtily, "who has dared instruct you to address gentlemen of our quality? Take his name," he said to Inouye, but the man disappeared, and they passed in.

Kano remembered the way, and, arriving at the house where they had met before, he inquired for Sanjo. He found, however, that this was the residence of Iwakura, and requested to be announced. After waiting a few moments, he found himself in the presence of the man who was one of the chief instruments in the re-organization of the empire.

"I am glad to see you, Mr. Councillor," said the kuge, "and you come at an opportune time. Some of us who are interested in the present movement, were going to meet later on. But I will request them to come as soon as possible." He clapped his hands, and gave some directions to the kneeling attendant. Presently a handsome screen was brought in and placed behind Kano; then he heard the opening of the sho ji behind the screen, and surmised that the meeting would be attended by a person of so exalted a rank as to be invisible to him.

Iwakura entertained his visitors in that charming manner, peculiar to the highbred Japanese. It appeared only a few minutes to Kano, when norimono began to arrive, and he and his friend were presented to the possessors of names, familiar to every Japanese, high or low. Ichijo, Nijo, Higashi Kuze,[81] all historic names, appeared. At last a norimono arrived, and Iwakura himself hastened to receive this visitor, who, with his attendants was ushered into the room behind. The other kuge kept up their conversation, but Kano noticed from the terms of self-debasement, and the frequent drawing of the breath, that the last caller must be, indeed, near to the throne. At last Iwakura reappeared, and took his seat.

"My lords," he said, "we have the unexpected but very gratifying pleasure of having as visitor the man who really started the movement which led to such surprising results. Mr. Kano is the trusted Councillor of our friend Mori of Nagato, and this gentleman, Mr. Inouye, he tells me, is his right hand. He has also informed me, while waiting for your lordships to arrive, that he has a thousand brave and devoted samurai at hand, ready to do His Majesty's bidding, and declares himself ready to answer any question it may please your lordships to ask."

Five minutes passed in performing the prostrations incident to this introduction, and Nijo, as the oldest of the kuge present, spoke:—

"I do not understand quite, Mr. Councillor, why the peace of the Gosho should be interrupted. His Lordship Iwakura tells us that you are the cause, and I doubt not that you have good reasons. At the same time, I protest that all these proceedings are highly improper, and that there is no precedent for them. I am told that the barbarians are at our door. Well, so they were six hundred years ago;[82] but His Majesty, as in duty bound, visited the shrine at Isé,[83] and implored the aid of the divine ancestors. The result is well-known. But the Gosho was not disturbed. To guard his country properly, His Majesty needs repose and contemplation. We like it not, Mr. Councillor, that his sacred presence should be disturbed."

Kano and Inouye bowed low, and were silent. After some moments of decorous silence, the kuge next in years spoke:—

"I agree with my lord Nijo. Why does not the Shogun expel the barbarians, as is his duty? The Court has ordered him to do so, and he has replied that he will do it as soon as the necessary preparations are made. So that matter is settled, it seems to me. I do not see what Mori, Shimadzu, and other captains have to do with it. His Majesty issues his commands to the Shogun who executes them reverently. These proceedings are highly improper, as my Lord Nijo said. If Mori desires any favor from the Fount of All Honor, let him apply to Iyemochi, and when his request, properly endorsed, reaches us through the proper channel, it will be considered and answered in due time."

It was now Sanjo's turn. "I have listened, my lords, with profound satisfaction to the lessons drawn from the ripe experience of my seniors. But I submit that our visitors be heard, since, having the misfortune to be mere soldiers, they may not be able to appreciate to the full extent the wisdom concentrated within the Council of Kuge."

At this appeal to their forbearance, the kuge bowed, and Kano, seizing his fan, began in a low but distinct voice:—

"I feel deeply, my lords, my own unworthiness, and appreciate the honor of being admitted to this august assembly." Here he prostrated himself, and remained fully three minutes, his head resting upon his outstretched hands. He then recovered his position, and continued:—

"Only a few years ago the country of the gods was at peace, thanks to Tenshi Sama and his intercession with the divine ancestors, and the repose of the Son of Heaven was undisturbed. Suddenly black ships appeared near the capital of the Tokugawa, and, being ordered to withdraw, refused to obey this reasonable behest. What did Tokugawa do? Smite the disobedient barbarians and hurl them back to their own desolate country? No! *Tokugawa was afraid.* The strangers departed but returned with reinforcements the next year. There had been ample time to call upon the clans to prepare for their visit, but *Tokugawa was afraid.* The Go rojiu pretended to be unprepared, and conceded all that the barbarians saw fit to ask. It was not much, but it was only the beginning of their demands. Four years later they asked more. They wanted land and the Tokugawa sold what was not his to sell. It was only a few tsubo,[84] in a poor fishing village, but it was soil of the country of the gods, part of the inheritance of the Son of Heaven. What did the divine ancestors say about this alienation of their sacred soil? My lords, you lay the blame of the disturbance of the sacred bosom upon me. I and my clan are ready to expiate our sin, if by doing so we can restore peace to the Light of our Day, to Tenshi Sama. But that peace can be restored only by placating His Majesty's ancestors, when they receive back their own."

Unconsciously, for Kano was not acting but meant every word he said, he stopped and allowed time for his words to sink into their breasts. No one lost his decorum, still, a movement of the fan, or a readjustment of the haori, betrayed the uneasiness of the kuge.

Kano resumed suddenly, with a slightly elevated voice:

"Aye, the divine ancestors must be placated, peace must be restored within the sacred walls of the Gosho, but the barbarians must be expelled before it can be accomplished. Hark ye! my lords. Myriads of samurai have come to this capital, and there is but one shout: Sonno-Joï! Revere the Emperor! Expel the foreigners! The breeze from the ocean gently fans our cheeks, so long as the gods look placidly down, while we, their humble servants, pay them our dues in respectful homage. But sometimes we fail in our duty. The breeze turns into a wind, the wind into a tai-fu,[85] and it sweeps all before it, the hovel of the laborer and the roof of the temple. What mortal can bid it refrain? The Yamato Damashii is the lovable zephyr of our country, but the presence of these insolent barbarians has converted it into a mighty wind. Hark ye, my lords, do you hear it swell? Sonno Joï! It is turning into a tai-fu now!"

Assuming the plaintive and appealing voice to which the language lends itself so well, Kano continued as if in self-commune:—

"We heed it not. The storm centres in our beloved land where the sun rises, but there is no rift in the clouded sky. The sun smiles upon the myriads of ships, cleaving the blue waters, and hurrying to the shores of our land. It is one long procession. Their spies have told the barbarians in their inhospitable regions of the one country where the gods love to dwell. From tens of rude, insolent men, they have increased to hundreds; they are now thousands and will soon be myriads. Tokugawa is no longer a vassal of Tenshi Sama, he is a servant to men scarce better than brutes. Hyogo and Osaka, are in their possession. The two roads to the sacred capital are crowded with them. Ye gods! will ye not at least preserve the Gosho and your child? They press against the wall, it gives way. Where is the peace and contemplation of the sacred enclosure now!"

His sighing voice melted into the silence, when in a strident tone that made them start, he concluded:—

"No! Sonno Joï roars out of a myriad throats. Myriads of brawny hands clasp the swords of Japan. Tenshi Sama has spoken through his brave miya and kuge. Clan after clan marches on, sun of victory for Yamato Damashii has come forth from behind the clouds and inspired Dai Nippon's sons. The Tokugawa has paid the penalty of treason; the barbarians have fled before the edge of the Soul of Samurai. Peace is restored and flowers innumerable and of brilliant colors delight the eye. After the tempest calm. Not that treacherous, oppressive air, forerunner of disaster. But the bright atmosphere which succeeds the storm as surely as prosperous peace will follow the tempest raging now, and which is the punishment for our neglect of duty."

XVIII
FLIGHT

SOLEMN was the scene, after Kano had concluded his address. He himself was prostrate once more, and remained in that position for more than five minutes, while not even the rustling of a silk hakama disturbed the silence. They sat like men of wax, immovable and serene. There was a rustling of silk behind the screen, it was removed, and a gentleman on whose haori appeared the imperial crest entered. All prostrated themselves, and he answered with a dignified bow. One of his attendants brought a cushion, and when he had squatted down, he said:

"Rise, Mr. Councillor."

Kano and Inouye obeyed.

"We have heard your statement and we approve of Mori's loyalty as expressed by you. Your report will receive our early attention and will be submitted to the proper authority. Fear not, son of Nagato, Tenshi Sama and our ancestors are keeping guard. Now go! You will receive our orders. Tomomi,[86] see to it that these gentlemen are refreshed." He bowed slightly and left the room. The other kuge followed as if they were glad to get away, and only Sanjo and Iwakura remained.

The latter ordered refreshments, and when they were brought, said: "Mr. Kano, I, and I suppose my lord Sanjo, are highly pleased. We have been in the minority, and have been in grave danger of our lives. But you have converted the miya nearest to the throne, and whatever happens, he is beyond danger, and a most powerful ally. Still, our council is large; and if Tokugawa replaces the present commandant by one who will make his authority felt, we shall be just where we were before."

"My lords, may I speak freely? I do not ask safety for myself. My life is worthless, but my cause and my clan are dear to me. Promise me that if I exceed the limits of propriety, or if what I say appears to you as high treason, you will permit me to let me expiate my transgression alone, and that it shall never go beyond these walls. My young friend will share my doom, so that the secret will remain locked up between you."

Both Iwakura and Sanjo bowed assent.

Kano after thanking them, said:—"Imperial orders are issued over His Majesty's sign manual, and the tenor of those orders depends naturally upon the sympathy of the kuge in charge. Could not a change be effected by which it was placed within the hands of one favorable to the cause of Japan?"

Iwakura looked at Sanjo and shook his head. "Impossible," he said. "The sign manual is held for life by one appointed by Tenshi Sama upon the request of a majority of the council. No," he repeated, "that can not be done."

"In that case," suggested Inouye, speaking before Kano could commit himself, "can not his Majesty be induced to ride to Hakone and drive the foreigners into the ocean. This would call forth such a host as Dai Nippon has never seen. There would be no danger, no risk even, for I am sure that the barbarians would not await the approach of such an army. They would take ship and depart, with the conviction that Dai Nippon was opposed to their presence."

"That might be done," said Sanjo, approvingly. "Send me an official letter signed with the seal of your clan and containing that request, and I shall submit it to the Council. But do it at once, and while the impression made by Mr. Kano is vivid. Let there be no delay."

"If your lordships will order one of your servants to go with us, the letter shall be written at once," replied Kano, preparing to depart. As they were leaving, a gentleman approached followed by a page. "Are these the gentlemen from Nagato?" he inquired. Being assured of their identity, he took a long package from the page and severing a cord, presented one to Kano and one to Inouye. "His Imperial Highness Prince Arisugawa bids you accept these as a token of his good will," he said. Both prostrated themselves and lifted the present to their forehead. When they arrived home, they found each a costly sword.

The letter was written and submitted to the Council. Kano's address must have made a deep impression, for he was informed in a private communication from Sanjo that his suggestion had been adopted, and orders had been issued to make the necessary preparations. At this time the fate of the foreigners in Japan hung by a thread.

Of all the clans of the Tokugawa family,—Iyeyasu had endowed his sons with ample estates,—all but Aidzu seemed as if stricken with palsy at the storm raging about them. But Aidzu, in its mountain home, had preserved its manhood, and despatched to Kyoto a man of penetration and dauntless courage. Shortly after taking command, the guards at the palace gates were quadrupled, and all ingress and egress prohibited, except under a most severe system of passports, obtained from the commandant himself.

On the 30th of September, 1863, Kano was sitting in his room overlooking the accounts of the clan, when Ito and Inouye entered hurriedly. There was no diminution of the salutations, and both waited until the Councillor spoke.

Kano, however, saw at once that something important had occurred, and he simply requested them to speak.

"Your lordship," said Ito, "there is something in the air. The commandant of the castle has issued orders to the people to close their houses and keep within, on penalty of being cut down. Armed patrols are in every street, and strong bodies of Aidzu men have taken up positions near the palace." At this moment an officer of the guard at the gate entered, and beckoned to Kano, who rose angrily and demanded if he had forgotten his manners. His explanation, however, seemed to satisfy the Councillor, for he said: All right, and hurried out. Presently he returned accompanied by seven gentlemen, among whom Ito and Inouye recognized Sanjo and Iwakura.

Rigidly observant of the salutations the company was at last seated, when Karassu Maru remarked:

"Mr. Councillor, I hope Mori's larder is well supplied, for I am afraid you are going to have us as your guests for some time."

Kano bowed and calling a servant ordered dinner to be prepared, when Sanjo spoke.

"My lord Karassu Maru chooses an odd time for pleasantry, but I am afraid, Mr. Councillor, that there is more truth in what he says than can be agreeable to you or us. The Council has honored myself and the gentlemen with me, with a decree of banishment."

Perturbed as he was, Kano bowed, and said simply:—I hope that it may please your lordships to accept the hospitality of Mori such as it is, but which is freely offered. Permit me to look after the safety of your lordships.

He went to the quarters of the commandant. "Have all the men under arms, and prepare to defend the gates. See that no man bearing the Tokugawa crest enters upon your life. Admit all stragglers, but no one is permitted to leave the yashiki except on written order over my seal. See that the arms and equipments are in proper order, for at five o'clock we march. Any disobedience will be punished most severely. Is this understood?"

"It is."

"Very well. Send for Mr. Hattori."

"He is in my room now."

Kano entered. "Hattori," he said, "we have received a severe check, but there is no time to explain. Ride for your life to Nagato, and inform Mori that seven kuge have been banished, and will accept his hospitality. Do not let him entertain the idea of changes in the rooms of the palace, but tell him that we shall be there almost as soon as you. As you pass by, engage rooms in the usual temples."

Hattori at once ordered a horse. Satisfied that there would be no delay, Kano sent for Ekichi:

"Dress as a boy of the common people," he said. "In a few minutes Mr. Fujii will give you a basket of eggs, and tell you their price. Then go slowly to the castle; notice closely everything you see, and report to me. Try to sell your eggs to the soldiers of the guard, but be careful that they do not suspect you. Be back by about four."

The boy was ready in a few minutes, and the Councillor himself saw him through the gate and gave him the pass word. He then returned to his guests, and informed them that they would leave for Choshiu at five.

While they were eating their dinner, Karassu Maru entertained the company, this was the time for relaxation, and his remarks elicited not unfrequently peals of laughter.

"I think that Honami is to blame for the whole thing. He came to me this morning, and said:—

"'What do you think? I am going to buy some rabbits.'

"It did not interest me very much, but for the sake of politeness, I asked: 'where?'

"'Oh!' he said, 'I have seen some beauties in Karassu Maru cho.'[87]

"I thought that he was indulging in personalities, and said:

"'You don't take me for a rabbit-warren do you?'

"'You? No; I wish you were.'"

Shouts of laughter greeted this sally, and the speaker laughed as heartily as the others. "Well," he continued, "I grew tired of his interesting conversation, and remarked that the rabbits might be waiting for him. This suggestion seemed to strike him, for away he trotted.

"He was not gone long before he came back in a great temper, and begged me to go with him to the gate, because they would not let him pass. He had told the guard, he said, that he had a very important appointment, but they would not listen to reason." There was a dangerous glitter in Karassu Maru's eye, as he continued: "I thought that the guard might have taken liberties with a kuge, and was going to give him a lesson in politeness. But when we came to the gate, an officer stepped out and said: 'Pardon me, my lord, but I am under orders to let no one pass. The Council is in session and your lordship will soon know the reason. I am compelled to escort you to your house.' The fellow was serious enough, and under guard of a dozen men I returned, Honami in his chair asking constantly about his rabbits. I had no stomach for them then."

XIX
BATTLE AND DEFEAT

It was a sullen procession which filed out of Choshiu's yashiki on that 30th of September, and it was well for the Tokugawa that no armed opposition was offered to them. Twelve hundred deeply insulted samurai could make sad havoc among any force, and these men hoped for the fray. They had marched in close ranks with seven norimono, well guarded between them. Kano was on horseback and had assumed command. He, too, had thought of the possibility of a conflict; but Ekichi had discovered that Satsuma had also been expelled, and that Choshiu would have to face the united power of Tokugawa. Loyalty to his clan, and the responsibility for the safety of the kuge imposed self-restraint; but they did not prevent him from being exasperated.

Past Fushimi[88] they marched, and on to Osaka where they remained over night. The next morning they stopped at Hyogo; it was eight days after they had left Kyoto when they were within their own province, and shortly after Mori in his state dress received the highly honored guests, and bade them make themselves at home.

Kano heard that Sawa had disappeared. That was well. Choshiu's samurai might not have liked to see the Tokugawa crest among them, and the blood of such a poor worthless creature, could not further the cause. But Choshiu thirsted for vengeance, and drilling went on from morning till night. Nagato was an armed camp.

Thus passed the winter and spring of the year 1864. Kano heard that the number of rônin multiplied at a frightful rate, and that many were congregating in the suburbs of Kyoto. Several young samurai applied for leave of absence, and, when they received a refusal, sent in their resignations and disappeared.

The men were exasperated. On the 4th of August a courier from Kyoto brought news which caused Kano to call an extra meeting of the Council. When they had come together, Kano informed them that in the beginning of July a body of rônin had petitioned Tenshi Sama to remove the decree of arrest from Mori, and to recall the seven kuge and restore them to honor; but the Council of the Gosho, now wholly under the influence of Aidzu had not even vouchsafed a reply. Several hundred Choshiu men had joined the rônin, and were preparing to march upon Aidzu.

This was serious news. What if Aidzu, in triumph at its success, should secure a decree of *Choteki*[89] against Mori from the servile court. That must be prevented at any cost! Kano and Hattori were commissioned to proceed in all haste to Kyoto, and to restrain their clansmen. They arrived at the capital on the 15th, and, appealing to the loyalty of their men, succeeded in bringing them back under Choshiu's banner.

Aidzu did not appreciate this self-control. On the 19th a Court messenger delivered a notification at the yashiki that Mori was to be punished for contumacy, and that Tokugawa Keiki[90] would command the loyal army commissioned to enforce the Court's order.

Kano and Hattori deliberated long and earnestly. There was not much choice. It was either to submit to punishment, which would strike their innocent lord the hardest of all, or trust to the spirit of unrest and leave the decision to the sword. The latter alternative was chosen, and Kano prepared a proclamation. He demonstrated the justice of his cause and mentioned the crimes committed by the Tokugawa since the arrival of Perry; he called upon the samurai of Japan to aid him in punishing Aidzu, who was desecrating the private grounds of Tenshi Sama, and implored the pardon of the Son of Heaven "for creating a disturbance so near the wheels of the Chariot."

The number of Choshiu men had increased to 1300. Kano had divided his men in three divisions, and, at dawn of the 20th of August, marched to the attack. His intention was to surround the flower garden of the palace where Aidzu's troops were encamped. They were opposed by the samurai of Aidzu who had been reenforced by those of Echizen, Kuwana, Hikone, and other Tokugawa clans. There were some cannon and muskets; but most of the men were in armor, and trusted to the keen native sword. With terrible odds against them, and no clan coming to their assistance, Choshiu maintained the fight for two days. A native historian states that 811 streets, 18 palaces, 44 large yashiki, 630 small yashiki, 112 Buddhist temples, and 27,000 houses were destroyed. The same historian says: "The city, surrounded by a ninefold circle of flowers, entirely disappeared in one morning in the smoke of the flames of a war fire. The Blossom Capital became a scorched desert." The end was such as might have been expected. The Choshiu men were utterly defeated. Thirty-seven men were taken prisoner and beheaded in prison. Kano died in battle, and his body was probably cremated, for it was not found.

When the fugitives began to arrive in Nagato, there was almost a panic among the samurai. Ito and Inouye, now recognized as leaders, restored quiet. It was not the defeat which had the effect of frightening men for whom pain nor death has any terror: it was the term *choteki*, which rendered their arm nerveless. It was only when Inouye proved to them that it was Aidzu and not Tenshi Sama who had inflicted this disgrace upon them that their courage returned together with their self-control.

The clan would soon stand in need of it. By Kano's order they had continued to fire upon vessels entering the Strait of Shimonoseki. They had Tenshi Sama's mandate to do so, and it had not been revoked. On the 5th of September a fleet of powerful vessels appeared, and bombarded Choshiu's forts. The men stood to their guns like heroes, but again the odds were against them. The batteries were blown about their ears, and when landing parties attacked the forts, individual daring backed by swords, could not stand before the withering fire of trained troops. The clan despatched Ito and Inouye to make peace, and the terms hard as they were, were accepted.

It was two days after the bombardment, and a meeting of the Council had been called in the great hall of the castle. Ito and Inouye, both Councillors now, were present. After all were seated, Ito opened the meeting.

"Gentlemen," he said, "there is little use in mourning for losses, since it will not repair them. But losses may be turned into an advantage, if we profit by the lessons we may derive from them.

"The foreign fleet which attacked us had such heavy metal, that our guns and gunners could not stand before it. It was a hail storm of iron and we went down before the blast. But when I saw that the barbarians were landing men, I thought that we were going to have our turn. They were but a handful, those barbarians, and man for man, our samurai would have made short work of them. But we could not get near them. They moved as one man and in the thickest of the fight a word of command was obeyed as if it was a machine instead of a body of men. It was their discipline and drill that defeated us, gentlemen, and we must acquire that same order and skill.

"We have met two foes, and twice we have been defeated. The barbarians will not molest us so long as we do not molest them, and, for the present at least, we shall leave that to other clans who may wish to pay for some experience. We stand face to face with another foe, and we are fighting for our very existence. Tokugawa would have us Choteki, gentlemen, and we must turn the tables upon them. We can do it, never fear! But first we must learn the drill and tactics from the barbarians that we may give Aidzu a surprise as the foreigners surprised us. For that purpose we must engage instructors and purchase arms. I now propose that Mr. Inouye be appointed with full authority to act in this matter, and that the treasurer of the clan furnish him with money."

"But," objected one of the older members, "the barbarian instructors will have to live among us; will they be safe? We do not want any more trouble with them now."

"Your lordship speaks well. We do not want any more trouble with them *now*. The next time we have trouble with them, it will not be we who pay the bills. They will be as safe here as in their own homes. Our samurai shall know why they are here. They shall know that we must dissemble; pretend that we are pleased with our defeat, and that we love the men who invaded our soil. But this dissembling will not last forever, and a time shall come when this defeat is wiped out. May we live to see it!"

The order was then passed and Ito resumed: "The next thing that *must* be done is to come to an understanding with Satsuma and the other Southern clans. Yes, I know, gentlemen, the dish is not palatable, but there is nothing for it but to eat it." A feud existed between Satsuma and Choshiu and to the older Councillors this advice was extremely repugnant. "We have no choice. Choshiu alone can not reduce the united Tokugawa Clans, and Tokugawa must be deposed unless we wish to see the barbarian our master. Satsuma, after all, is of our blood, and has the same interests. Tosa too, must join. I propose then that I undertake this disagreeable work; somebody must do it, and I do not suppose that any one cares for the honor."

There was a silence. At last one of the Councillors spoke: I suppose that Mr. Ito is right. Let it be as he wishes. I agree with him that of the two, Satsuma is preferable to the barbarians.

The order was entered upon the books and the council adjourned. The two friends left together. Inouye said he would start the next day.

"Have you any objection if I take Ekichi with me?"

Ito looked up, smiled, and said: "None at all."

XX
DRILLING

THE severe defeats suffered by Choshiu had reduced the number of samurai of the clan. After thinking deeply upon the matter, Ito proposed to the Council a measure which met with the most strenuous opposition, and, being earnestly supported by Inouye, was at last adopted with many an ominous shake of the head. It was, namely, that the ranks should be recruited from among the young and strong members of the people. The older members of the council urged, not unnaturally, that the samurai would never suffer such an infringement upon the privileges of their rank. Both Ito and Inouye had more confidence in the loyalty of the samurai, and they were right. The very best of foreign rifles had been purchased by Inouye and arrived in due time. Then the instructors came, and drilling went on from morning to night. The young men of the people vied with the samurai in zeal and enthusiasm, they were all equally and regularly paid and well treated. After some time artillery began to arrive, and a corps of men was detailed to learn gunnery. Among all the young men there was none more zealous than Ekichi. After a year's drill, when officers were appointed he was made a lieutenant.

In the shadow side of the dual part in the Japanese character, there is no passion so strong as that of revenge. Subterfuge, the most dastardly treachery, are praiseworthy and commendable, if they serve to obtain revenge for the killing of a near relation. The written constitution of old Japan (Legacy of Iyeyasu), prescribed:

"In respect to revenging injury done to master or father, it is granted by the wise and virtuous (sage)[91] that you and the injurer can not live together under the canopy of heaven.

"A person harboring such vengeance shall notify the same in writing to the Criminal Court; and although no check or hindrance may be offered to his carrying out his desire within the period allowed for that purpose, it is forbidden that the chastisement of an enemy be attended with riot.

"Fellows who neglect to give notice of their intended revenge are like wolves of pretext, and their punishment or pardon should depend upon the circumstances of the case."

Ekichi suspected Sawa. If he had been asked for the reason, he would have been at a loss, except that he had seen him at Kyoto on the day of the flight of the kugé. He had never liked the spy, and he had worshiped his father. The lesson of self-control, thoroughly mastered by him, enabled him to bend his mind upon his studies. But the moments which he allowed himself for relaxation, were spent in brooding upon revenge.

Inouye suspected it, and for that reason had taken him with him to Yokohama. While there he had found time to go to Kanagawa where he called upon the physician in his samurai dress. The family scarcely recognized their former houseboy who, in gratitude for former kindness, presented his late employer with a choice piece of lacquer. Inouye had watched Ekichi keenly during this visit, and had noticed the absolute self control with which he received the advances of the barbarians. At dinner, he simply imitated Inouye but with such perfect self-possession, that it seemed as if he had been using knife and fork all his life, although it was the first time he saw them.

At Yokohama, too, his face expressed no emotion at what he saw; only when in passing the hatoba, Inouye remarked that his father had worked here, the boy prostrated himself and saluted. He was utterly unconscious of the laughter of some rude barbarians. Inouye noticed, however, that he asked for the names in English, after he had heard him converse in that language.

When they returned to Nagato, he had asked to be enrolled in the army and his request was granted. Inouye had offered to teach him English, an offer which was gladly accepted, and he made such progress that he was able to read understandingly and to keep up a fair conversation.

The Tokugawa in the meanwhile was boasting of how the Shogun would annihilate Choshiu, and in 1865 Iyemochi himself took the field. The foreigners at Yokohama were permitted to witness the march of the redoubted troops. They came straggling by, as an eye-witness describes in bands of three or four, a motley array, with very little stomach for the business in hand. The same witness states that, upon arrival at Odawara[92] the majority of the higher samurai applied for leave of absence on account of sickness; whereupon they were told that they could go, but that their revenues would be taken from them, whereupon they recovered their health. They remained that year quartered at Kyoto and Osaka, for the Shogun did not care to lead such an army against a brave and desperate clan. He tried to induce other clans to join him, but they refused flatly.

Stung by the ridicule heaped upon them by Japanese and foreigner alike, the Tokugawa troops at last opened the campaign, in the summer of 1866. Instead of attempting to overwhelm the clan by sheer force of numbers, Iyemochi divided his army into three divisions, each of which was separately routed by Choshiu. This restored the prestige of the clan, while it ruined that of Tokugawa.

In every battle Ekichi had excelled for coolness and courage, and it was predicted that he would rise as his father had done before him. In the latter part of September the news was brought to Nagato that Iyemochi, the Shogun was dead. Shortly later it also became known that Tokugawa Keiki had succeeded, but by appointment from Tenshi Sama.

The death of Tenshi Sama Osahito,[93] better known by his posthumous name of Komei[94] Tenno, and the succession of his son Mutsuhito, then a boy of fifteen produced a great change. Ito and Inouye held frequent and long conferences, and the former was often absent from the clan.

Their own experience within Choshiu's narrow limits, had convinced them that they were on the right track. The whole strength of Choshiu's clan had been called out, and had repeatedly defeated the overwhelming forces of the Tokugawa; but it had been able to do so only after acquiring the principles of foreign art of war. Ito disliked and mistrusted the foreigners, whereas Inouye's experience as well as his strong power of discernment rather inclined him toward them. Both, however, were agreed in their love of their country; and both agreed that the Japanese must acquire every particle of knowledge in the possession of the barbarians. More than that: their manners, habits, and customs, must be studied and such as served in any way to strengthen the national life, must be introduced and adapted. But before anything could be done in that direction, the Tokugawa must be laid low. Nothing could possibly be done so long as a clan so degenerate was foremost in the country.

Ito went to Satzuma, and met OKubo, Saigo, and Terashima. In OKubo and Terashima he met men who felt and thought like he. Saigo, a splendid specimen of manhood, over six feet in height, was equally predisposed against the Tokugawa, but was not able to look beyond the clan. As there was no warrant against any of these men except those of the Choshiu clan, they moved to Kyoto, and the rebuilt capital again became a hotbed of intrigue.

Tokugawa Keiki declined the appointment of Shogun, but was compelled to accept. The councillors of the several Tokugawa clans were very well aware that their sun had set, and urged his appointment as of a man who was personally popular with the other clans. But Keiki perceived that the days of the Shogunate were past. It is not improbable that he himself perceived, as Ii Navsuke had done before, that united Japan only would be able to maintain its independence and such a Japan could not exist under two heads. He offered repeatedly to resign, but the Gosho had no liking for the idea of leaving its repose. The majority of the members clung to the ideas of Nijo. As to the boy emperor, he had no more voice than his father had had before him, or than Mori possessed within Choshiu's clan. In the regeneration of Japan, no help could be expected from Miya, Kuge, or Daimiyo, long since converted into puppets by the very duality of the national character. The men who undertook the work were unknown nobodies; but it was exactly by such men that the different clans had been ruled separately, and by combining together they could rule all the clans, that is Japan, collectively.

Strictly speaking, therefore, there was no vital change in the affairs of Japan so long as the government was nominally in the hands of a figurehead, and in reality in those of the samurai. In all these troubles, the people had no share, nor did they take any interest in them, except when their own personal interests were directly affected. In the eyes of the dominating class the people had no existence; and when, in the documents of those days the word "people" is used, it refers solely to the samurai.

Although Aidzu was still in possession of Kyoto, and in charge of the gates of the Gosho, the half-hearted orders of Keiki permitted the leaders of Satsuma and other clans to communicate with their friends within the Council, and once again the men who were for repose at any cost felt the ground moving from under their feet. They brought pressure to bear upon the Shogun, and he once again offered his resignation. It was accepted on the 9th of November, 1867, but upon condition that for the present he should continue the administration.

XXI
DOWN WITH TOKUGAWA!

GREAT events were expected when the year 1868 dawned. Couriers arrived daily at Nagato from Kyoto, and our two friends, as well as the banished kuge were in a fever of expectation. Ekichi had asked and obtained furlough, and had left for Kyoto. He was greatly attached to Inouye, and frequently forestalled his wishes, but in a quiet, unobtrusive way. He was, moreover, so sedate in his habits, that there was no cause for watching him. However much Ito and Inouye would have done for him for the sake of his late father, they felt that his future could be safely left to himself.

The two friends had taken dinner together on the 7th of January, when the galloping of a horse was heard, and the animal stopped evidently in front of the yashiki. After a slight delay, a servant appeared and announced Mr. Kano. A moment later Ekichi entered, somewhat flushed. They saluted, and Inouye who observed him closely, said:

"You came on horseback and evidently had a long journey. Have you had dinner?"

"No, sir, I did not wish to loiter on the road."

A servant was ordered to serve dinner to the guest. After he had finished, Inouye resumed:

"You bring important news, do you not?"

"Satsuma, Tosa, and some other clans took possession of the Gosho, four days ago, and Arisugawa no Miya is guardian on His Majesty."

Inouye clapped his hands. When his attendant appeared, he told him to go to the castle, and request the kuge to honor him with a call. Ito, who had been charged with the command of the army, rose and said: "Shall we march in the morning?"

"Yes," was the reply, "that will be best."

The two friends had so often considered what they would do when this time should arrive, that no further consultation was necessary. Ito went first to the most active Councillor, and explained to him what had happened; he then proceeded to the barracks, and gave orders that the army was to march at six in the morning. When he returned, he found the kuge, highly pleased at the prospect of their speedy return. They knew that, with Arisugawa as adviser, Tenshi Sama would restore them to honor, and Mori would be exculpated. Indeed, at four o'clock in the morning a messenger arrived bringing the official papers.

The two Councillors breakfasted with the kuge. During the meal, Ito said:

"We must make hurried marches, gentlemen. Tokugawa will not submit peaceably. If our friends prevail, it means the ruin of the Tokugawa men; hence I expect we shall have trouble."

The army marched out, leaving only a sufficient number of men to guard the territory of the clan. It was now that the difference between samurai and an army on the march could be best observed. The men stepped out evenly in close ranks, and easily, and without apparent fatigue performed a two days' journey. The kuge were surprised. Ito and Inouye explained what had been done, and the reason for it. Whereas the daimiyo had never traveled to Kyoto in less than seven days, the Choshiu men arrived at their yashiki within four days from the time they left Nagato.

The kuge were escorted to the Palace. Here they found that an entirely new order prevailed. The allied clans guarded the gates, but permitted free ingress and egress to all samurai except such as bore the Tokugawa crest. An imperial decree had been issued abolishing the office of Shogun, and declaring that the government would be conducted by the imperial court. Negotiations were being conducted with Keiki to arrive at an equitable settlement.

Brought up as he had been as the son of Mito, Keiki had always trusted to his councillors, and was quite as ignorant of affairs as Mori. He has been accused of vacillation, but personally he was not consulted at all. Answers, of which he knew nothing, were given in his name and under his seal. It was quite natural that among his councillors there should be two parties, the one advocating submission, the other resistance. The answer depended upon the majority among his councillors.

At last it was decided by his advisers that he should leave Kyoto and withdraw to Osaka. He was escorted by the two clans of Aidzu and Kuwana, both intensely attached to the house of Iyeyasu, and unspoiled. Their leaders urged, and almost compelled Keiki to fight. Himself possessed of patriotic impulses, he refused.

The new government at Kyoto dreaded war; not from fear, but on account of the probable consequences. Sanjo and Iwakura had been reinstated and were often in conference with Ito, Inouye, Goto, OKubo, and Saigo. It was plainly evident that the government could not be carried on without revenue, and the Court possessed nothing but a pittance allotted to it from Tokugawa's superfluity. If war should follow, Tokugawa had resources, while the court had none. Even at present the Court depended entirely upon the generosity of the clans which had been instrumental in effecting the revolution.

But the ex-Shogun or his party had also very good reasons for avoiding civil war. It was they who would be Choteki this time, and every Japanese has a horror of that word. Besides, the Tokugawa clans were divided among themselves. Echizen and Owari had openly declared for Tenshi Sama, and had, in fact aided in ousting Aidzu. There was thus every prospect of peace, and the Court, to facilitate negotiations, despatched the daimiyo of Echizen and Owari, to offer the Tokugawa clan a fair share in the government.

Keiki wished to accept; indeed, he was most anxious to wash his hands of all interference with politics, but Aidzu and Kuwana would not have it. They expected to restore the old order of things, and Keiki escorted by the two clans, much against his will, set out upon the return journey to Kyoto.

The army of the allied clans was small, being almost completely composed of Satsuma and Choshiu men. But these men were excellently drilled, for Satsuma, too, had had a lesson from the barbarians, and profited by it. The loyal army, that is the army of the allied clans had taken a strong position at Fushimi. The Yodo river connects this town with Osaka, with a good road on each bank. The Tokugawa forces marched by both banks, and were received by a well-directed artillery fire. The rice fields prevented them from deploying and, as they understood nothing but a hand to hand mêlée, they had no chance in taking a strong strategic position. Three days they attempted to carry Fushimi and failed. Then they broke and fled, pursued by the victorious imperialists.

Ekichi had commanded a battery in this battle, and had again distinguished himself by his calmness and steadiness under fire. When the battle was over, he went to his commanding officer, and begged to be detailed for the pursuit. His request was granted, and soon he was among the foremost of the imperialists. It was noticed that he did not use his sword, except in self-defense. Half-way toward Osaka the pursuers were commanded to halt.

The imperial forces were not strong enough to cope with those of the Tokugawa, and orders were sent to the loyal clans to send reinforcements. From all parts of the South and West samurai hurried to support the Tenshi Sama's cause and it was not long before the loyal army set out in pursuit.

Keiki had escaped from Aidzu by departing for Yedo on one of his steamships; upon his arrival there he sent in his submission, but the mountain clans would not obey his orders. It is odd that he should not have taken his seal with him; if these same orders had been issued over his seal, there is no doubt that Aidzu and Kuwana would have submitted. But personal government had for centuries been unknown in Japan. If Mori, personally, should have given an order to Choshiu, nobody would have paid any attention to it; and if an order to exactly the opposite effect had appeared over his seal, it would have been obeyed at once.

We shall now return to our friends.

While the Choshiu forces, escorting the recalled kuge were marching toward Kyoto, Ito remained behind, quietly biding his time. After the battle of Fushimi was fought and Keiki had embarked for Yedo, the Tokugawa officials deserted their posts and fled. Ito at once went to the administration building, and declared himself governor for his Majesty Tenshi Sama. He took over the government, and prevented lawlessness.

Kobe, a part of the beach in the immediate vicinity of Hyogo had been opened to foreigners, and Ito declared it his purpose to protect them. The same policy had been adopted by those who advised the young Emperor. Japan was never in a worse position to defy a foreign power and her leaders were aware of the fact. One and all they hated the barbarians, but they loved their country more. They had roughly outlined a policy which was to make of Japan a united and great country, and that object they lost never out of sight.

At Yedo the Aidzu clan made a stand at the beautiful temple at Uyeno (Pron. Oo-way-no). Here Ekichi was in the van. Both parties fought with desperate courage, but Tokugawa lost. Among the dead was Kano Ekichi, the son of the dead leader.

XXII
CONCLUSION

THIRTY-SEVEN years have passed since this story opened. It is in the month of May, 1895, and two men are sitting at a hibachi in an upper room in Shinagawa, formerly a suburb of Yedo, now a part of the city of Tokyo. The men were hale and hearty, but their gray hair, bordering on white, showed that they were beyond middle age. Their hair was cut after our fashion, but one wore a straggling beard, while the other's snow-white moustache showed off to advantage his small mouth.

The room where they were sitting was at the back of the second story of a house, which, apparently at least was of our cottage style of architecture. If one had pressed the electric bell, and entered it, he would not have seen anything except what might be expected in the home of a well-to-do American or European. He might have noticed the taste displayed by the owner, and the quiet, unobtrusive elegance, but it would not have caused him to suspect that he was in the house of a Japanese.

The whole of the lower floor, except the kitchen and servants' rooms, was such as one might have expected in an opulent American or English city. The upper story, however, retained the native simplicity, save that walls, instead of the light, airy sho ji, helped to support the roof. The prospect from every side was lovely, for the house stood on one of the bluffs, bordering the former Tokaido. That highway was there still, but its glory has departed. Every hour, and sometimes more frequently, trains run between Yokohama and Tokyo, and thousands of passengers mingle daily in the large waiting-rooms and in the depot at Shinbashi. There the former daimiyo comes in actual contact with the ninzoku, and the kuge of old stands by the side of the merchant.

The front of the house gives a view of the bay, lovely at high tide but disagreeable when the ebb exposes mud-banks extending three miles from the shore. It will not be long before the government will perceive the value of this land, and the eyesore will disappear. If Rome could have been built in a day, these Japanese would have done it.

If Ito looks from the windows on the right, toward Shinagawa, his eye must fall upon the handsome residence of Mori, where the son of his former lord now leads a life of quiet elegance. He is well satisfied with it. When Ito, now higher in rank than his former lord, calls to pay his respects as he often does, the same relation seems to exist as in former days. Again Ito is the simple samurai, his lord the daimiyo, and in both there is a secret longing for the days that are past. But when they look about them that longing ceases, and they are glad and proud of what they see.

From the windows in the left, Ito looks upon Tokyo, now grown into one of the world cities. Has it changed in these thirty-seven years? To be sure it has, but not oppressively. As we walk through the streets where dwell the people, we notice that they are wider and cleaner; but the houses are still as they were before, although there is evidence of greater prosperity. In Ginza, the street of the large shops, we see a mixture of the occident and orient, not altogether pleasant; houses built in foreign style, divided into Japanese rooms or Japanese houses with imitation foreign stores. Still it is all Japanese, that is, we can not, even for a moment, lose sight of the fact that we are in Japan.

"BUT THE HOUSES ARE STILL AS THEY WERE BEFORE."

But it is within the former castle grounds that a great change is noticeable; especially at Sakura, near the spot where Ii Naosuke paid with his head the hatred of Mito. Where his yashiki stood is an elegantly built edifice of brick, a girls' school, formerly the polytechnic, and facing the moat are a number of villas. In the first of these dwelt Sanjo during his life; next to it is the house once occupied by Shimadzu, the head of the Satsuma clan, and up the hill is the palace of Arisugawa, now in mourning, for its head died some months ago.

It is quite evident that two strong forces are working in Japan. The leaders of the people are sincere in their desire to conform more and more to occidental ideals, whereas the people are striving strenuously to return to their former habits and customs in domestic life. Both parties are impelled by the same motive, love of country. But the leaders have more experience and a wider horizon. They have been abroad, and judge occidental life, with all its virtues and vices by the results which they produced. The people know nothing of foreigners, except of such with whom they come into contact, and they have no love for them.

Thus, as an old friend expressed it to me, all our modern improvements such as tend toward enhancing the nation's greatness and wealth, have been assimilated. Japan, to-day, could no more do without railroads, than we could do without them. It is the same with telegraph and telephone and other inventions where steam or electricity are the motive. The army and navy have been organized according to the highest standards, and will keep pace with the best of the world. Industries have been and are being organized, and receive careful protection from the government. But in the home life, the Japanese have turned back.

"The luxury of your homes," said my friend, "tends toward enervating the race. We do not need your furniture; it is expensive and inelegant. We sleep upon our futon as well as you do upon your spring mattress. In your clothing you are the slaves of a thing you call fashion, and every year or oftener you are called upon to pay tribute to it. Who ever heard of anything so foolish? Our clothing keeps us cool in summer, and hot in winter. It is inexpensive, becoming, and leaves our limbs to their natural action; what more do we want? As to your food, I acknowledge that a meat diet is more strengthening than our usual bill of fare, and most of us indulge in it once a day. But to prepare dishes merely to tickle the palate, is both foolish and wicked. We want no waste. That is the reason why I prefer dressing in haori, hakama, and Kimono, and why I prefer to live in a Japanese house. If I, or any other Japanese, visit your country, we conform with your customs and habits, because we do not wish to give offense. When you come here, you bring your customs and habits with you, and parade them before us, regardless if you give offense or not. I think in doing so, you act wrongly or at least in bad taste."

"You believe in doing at Rome as the Romans do," I said smiling. "But surely one can not always do so. Excuse me, but most of your dishes are absolutely repugnant to me."

"What does that prove, but that you are a slave to your stomach. Do you remember when we first met? It is a long time ago, but I shall never forget it. The impression of that day is still vivid within me. I had heard that a barbarian had come to live in our next door yashiki, and I wondered what sort of an animal he was. My father had told me I must be very civil when I should see you, and, of course, there was nothing for it but to mind. I had come from school when I heard steps behind me and then somebody grabbed me and I saw you. It was well that I did not wear my swords at that time, or we should not be talking here, and Japan would have paid another indemnity. You don't know the fury you raised in me at your unceremonious introduction. Well, you dragged me in your yashiki, and placed bread, butter and sugar before me. Do you remember that, when your kadzukai came in, I asked him what those things were, and what you wanted me to do with them? He told me they were bread, oil from the cow, (niku no abura), and sugar, and were there for me to eat. Talk of repugnant! It was nauseous to me to think of such a thing as eating 'oil from the cow.' But when I am in America now, I enjoy my butter and sometimes help myself twice."

"That may be," I replied, "but for the life of me, I could not eat your raw fish, and many other dishes."

"Pshaw! It is on account of an imagination which we call prejudice. You don't possess the nerve to try them, and if you did from some reason, for instance false shame, they would probably upset your stomach. You could not turn my stomach in those days, child though I was, but sometimes you tried me pretty severely. When I came home that first evening, I told my father all about you, and if you had heard my description, I do not think that you would have felt flattered. But he told me to cultivate your acquaintance, and his word was law.

"It took me sometime to grow accustomed to—to—, well, I shall draw it mild, to your lack of manners and of good breeding. But then, as my father explained to me, you were only a barbarian, and without any education; and you were, or tried to be, kind; I appreciated that. So you taught me English, and I taught you Japanese, and you tested my self-control by the funny mistakes you made. Let me see how long is that ago? Twenty-six years? How long will it be before you can speak Japanese, do you think?"

"Come, that is rather rough on me," I laughed. "I find I can get along very well."

"Yes? I always did admire my fellow-countrymen. They have now another claim to my regard. I speak in Japanese with you for the sake of old times; but, do you know that I sometimes need all my equanimity to bear with the way in which you murder our language. Sometimes you use expressions as if I were your superior in rank; that is all right and proper; but when, a moment late, you hurl a word at my head fit only for a coolie or a servant, I admire the perfect control I have of my temper. No!" he continued slowly and looking thoughtfully at me, "I don't think you will ever learn Japanese."

"I am satisfied with what I know," I replied, "but if my use of your tongue shocks your ear, I am willing to converse in English, and I promise you that I shall not criticize either your pronunciation or grammar."

He bowed ceremoniously and replied: "No, thank you! When I am in the United States, or in England, I speak English and try to act as regardless of the feelings of others as your fellow Anglo-Saxons act. As soon as I begin to think in English, it seems as if I forget that I am a Japanese gentleman."

"You must have mastered our language better than I have yours, then, for when I speak in Japanese I can never bring myself to use those elegant circumlocutions which we call by a name which to us has an ugly sound."

This time it was my friend's turn to laugh. "Do you remember when poor Kato first came to see you? We were at our lessons, and he to do you honor had spent a few days in learning the phrases: 'I have heard of your famous name,' and 'I am happy to see your face.' He came in and recited those two sentences in very fair English, I thought. I see you jumping up yet. What a spitfire you were! Poor Kato! He did not know what to make of it. You roared: 'Now, what is the use of talking that way? You never heard of my name, for it is not famous, and you don't care about my face any more than I care about yours.' Kato's stock of English was exhausted, and he politely requested me to come to his assistance. Well, I had manners if you had not, so I told him that you were overpowered at the honor of his call, and that this was your manner to invite him to make himself at home."

"So that was the reason that fellow bored me until eleven o'clock. I owe you one for that!"

"Yes? We paid you foreigners well in those days, more than we could really afford, but most of you were worth the money. Not on account of the duties you performed, not always satisfactorily but generally to the best of your ability, but on account of the never failing amusement you afforded us. At a time when you thought yourself a fair Japanese scholar I have heard you criticized right before you, and you were as unconscious as a babe."

"Don't you think that you show by what you say the real difference between you and our race. By your own confession, I showed you kindness, and, my memory deceives me badly, or you reciprocated to some extent my friendship for you. Yet you could stand by and patiently listen to an adverse criticism of one who was your friend, and, instead of resenting it, as I would have done in a similar case, you could be amused by it."

"Ah! but you forget. At that time you were still an object of suspicion to us. Shimonoseki and Kagoshima were recent recollections, and we were eating humble-pie. It is different now. We know your strength and your weakness and we know also our own strength, and we can magnanimously condescend to treat you as our equals. At that time the whole nation dissembled; we hated you and every foreigner, although we treated you so as to flatter your conceit. It does not raise a people in its own eyes when it forces itself to discard, even for a time, its national pride, and pretend to honor those whom it despises and hates. I tell you, my old friend, I am proud of my country and of my people. We passed through a fiery ordeal, and came out purified. But I acknowledge also that the fire has left scars which only time can heal. We are growing better, not worse. The fact that we two still find pleasure in each other's company proves that we are better able to appreciate each other's good qualities, and that is a type of the feeling of Japan toward foreign nations."

NOTES

Meanings and Pronunciation of Japanese Words used in the Text.

1. Pron. Day-shee-mah, little island.
2. Pron. Nang-ah-sah-kee.
3. Pron. Shoh-goon. General-in-chief.
4. Pron. Die-mee-yoh. This word means Great Name.
5. Pron. Sah-moo-rye.
6. Pron. Yed-doh, now Tokyo (pron. To-kee-yoh), or Eastern Capital. Yedo was the capital of Old Japan, from 1600 to 1868.
7. Pron. Kee-yoh-toh, the real capital of Old Japan.
8. Pron. Ten-shee Sah-mah. Lord of Heaven.
9. Pron. Toh-koo-ngah-wah.
10. Pron. Ee-yay-yas.
11. Pron. Say-kee-gah-hah-rah.
12. Pron. Moh-ree.
13. Pron. Cho-shu, in the southwest part of the Island of Hondo, the mainland of Japan.
14. Pron. yash-kee.
15. Pron. Ee-yay-meets.
16. Pron. Moots'-shtoh.
17. Pron. hah-kah-mah, loose trousers, part of the dress reserved to knights and nobles.
18. Pron. kah-yah-kee, a hardwood.
19. Pron. show-jee.
20. Pron. ah-may.
21. Pron. hee-bat-chee, a charcoal brazier, to warm the hands or light the pipe.
22. Pron. keé-moh-noh.
23. Pron. Hie, hie! meaning "yes" or "coming".

24. I have translated the conversations in intelligible English. To give the forms of self-abasement of the speaker, and the titles of honor to the person addressed, would sound ridiculous to us.

25. Pron. On-nah Die-gah-koo, a book giving the rules for married women.

26. Pron. sah-kee.

27. Pron. Hat' toh ree.

28. Pron. mets' kay, an official spy, appointed by the Shogun government.

29. Pron. Go-roh-jiu (*u* the French sound), Hon. Great Council which issued all orders from the Shogun to the great Daimiyo.

30. Pron. Sah-wah.

31. Pron. noh-ree-moh-noh, a sort of sedan chair.

32. Pron. Ee-toh.

33. Pron. Toh-kie-doh, the great highway running from Tokyo to Kyoto.

34. Pron. Mee-toh and I-dzoo, two clans belonging to the Tokugawa family.

35. Pron. Ee-ee Nah-oh-skay, Daimiyo of Hikoni and regent of Japan, who was afterwards assassinated.

36. Pron. Ee-no-yay.

37. Pron. how-ree, a thin mantlet of crêpe, with the coat of arms worked on the back and sleeves.

38. Pron. Kee-ee, and Oh-wah-ree, the two estates taken from Choshiu and given to the sons of Iyeyasu.

39. Pron. Shtah nee eeroo.

40. Pron. Ay-kee-chee.

41. Pron. f'ton.

42. The legacy of Iyeyasu, the law book of Old Japan.

43. The plain, east of the Hakone Mountains which contains Yedo.

44. Pron. Nah-kah-sen-doh, another highway between Yedo and Kyoto. In the narrowest passes of both roads barriers were placed which no one could pass, except when provided with passports from the government.

45. Pron. roh-neen, a samurai who did not belong to a clan. The Yedo government held the clan responsible for the acts of its samurai.

46. Pron. Foo-jee, Kano's chief retainer.

47. Pron. Yah-doh-yah, an inn.

48. Pron. hee-yahk-show, literally peasant.

49. Pron. Kodz'kie.

50. Pron. ee-chee-roh-koo nee-chee, literally one-six-day. Until 1874 every fifth day was a holiday for the samurai; these days were the 1st, 6th, 11th, 16th, etc.

51. O before a name means honorable. Pron. O Kee-chee.

52. Pron. tah-tah-mee, thick rush mats.

53. Pron. ree-yoh, old Japanese coin equal to about $1.00.

54. Pron. neen-zoh-koo, a coolie or day laborer.

55. Pron. yah-shwee moh-noh, the name by which the Roman Catholics were known.

56. Issued Jan. 27, 1614.

57. Pron. Ty Coon. This is really a Chinese word and means Great Prince.

58. Pron. O Ee-shah-sahn.

59. Pron. nar-rah foo-doh! which may be translated by; Is that so?— You don't say so! and similar expressions.

60. Pron. hat'-to-bah, jetty or landing.

61. Pron. Ay-to.

62. Pron. Tay-rah-jee.

63. Pron. Kah-mee'-shee-moh.

64. Pron. sep' poo-koo, suicide by disemboweling, commonly called hara-kiri. Pron. hah-rah' kee-ree'.

65. Pron. Ee-yay-sah-dah.

66. Pron. Mee-toh. Of the three great Tokugawa families, Mito, Kii, and Owari, Mito, by a secret clause in Iyeyasu's will was debarred from succeeding as Shogun.

67. Pron. Koong-ay, court nobles, descendants from former emperors, who held the same position at the court as did the councillors in the clan.

68. The Court of Tenshi sawa.

69. Pron. Son-noh Joe-ee.

70. Saru-me (pron. sah roo may), an approbrious term used to express contempt and indignation.

71. Pron. Yah-mah-toh Dah-mash-yee.

72. Pron. Kah-ras-soo Mah-roo.

73. A kuge was of much higher rank than a daimiyo, and even of the Shogun. They did not mention the daimiyo by their estate, but by their family name.

74. Pron. Mee-yah, families accounted as Princes of the Blood. Most of them were nurtured like the daimiyo, and wholly unable to think for themselves.

75. Pron. Nee-joh, one of the leading Kuge families.

76. Pron. kah-kay-moh-noh, hanging scroll.

77. Pron. Shee-mad-zoo, family name of the lord of Satsuma.

78. According to Confucius.

79. This document is quoted in F. O. Adams' History of Japan.

80. Pron. Shee-moh-noh-say-kee.

81. Pron. Ee-chee-joe, Nee-joe, Hee-gash-ee Koo-zay.

82. Nijo refers to the repulse of the Tartars in A. D. 1281.

83. Pron. Ee-say.

84. Pron. tsoo-boh, a square measure.

85. Pron. ty-foo, our typhoon; lit. great storm.

86. A member of the Imperial family, addressing one of inferior rank of the same, uses the given name. Iwakura's given name was Tomomi.

87. There is a street of that name in Kyoto.

88. Pron. Foo-shee-mee.

89. Pron. Cho-tay-kee, *i. e.*, rebel against Tenshi Sama.

90. Pron. Kay-kee.

91. Confucius.

92. Pron. Oh-dah-wah-rah, a town at the foot of the Hakome range.

93. Pron. Oh-sah-shtoh.

94. Pron. Koh-may.

THE END

FOOTNOTES:

[A] It was the American fleet, under Commodore Perry, who was sent by President Millard Fillmore to make a treaty with Japan.

[B] In the month of September, 1854, a series of earthquakes began which lasted almost without interruption until the end of December. Twenty thousand houses and sixteen thousand fire-proof warehouses were destroyed in Yedo alone. Over 100,000 people were reported killed. Osaka and Hyozo were destroyed, and Kyoto suffered considerable damage.

[C] The Russian frigate *Diana*.

Milton Keynes UK
Ingram Content Group UK Ltd.
UKHW051023250324
439991UK00008B/999